WITNESS IN THE ACADEMY

VERSION 2

WITNESS IN THE ACADEMY
VERSION 2

A guide for graduate students, faculty, and those who minister with them

RICK **MATTSON**

InterVarsity GFM
635 Science Dr.
Madison, WI 53711
gfm.intervarsity.org

InterVarsity GFM is the Graduate and Faculty ministry of InterVarsity Christian Fellowship/USA: Planting and growing witnessing communities of graduate students and faculty committed to spiritual formation, community, evangelism and service, and the integration of faith, learning, and practice. Learn more at: www.gfm.intervarsity.org.

All Scripture quotations, unless otherwise indicated are taken from THE HOLY BIBLE, NEW INTERNATIONAL VERSION®, NIV® Copyright © 1973, 1978, 1984, 2011 by Biblica, Inc.™ Used by permission. All rights reserved worldwide.

While all stories in this book are true, some names and identifying information may have been changed to protect the privacy of individuals.

The publisher cannot verify the accuracy or functionality of website URLs used in this book beyond the date of publication.

ISBN: 9798387161247

Printed in the United States of America.

"As in every generation, we too live in a dark time and a broken world. But it is not for us to save the world. Christ has already acted to do that and promises in time to complete this salvation of all that he loves. We bear witness to this good, if improbable, message as we go out every day to invite students and faculty into this belief, this way of living, this world and life view, these communities of formation and witness and work — marked at their best by faith, hope, and (most powerfully) love."

　- Bobby Gross, Vice President | Graduate and Faculty Ministries InterVarsity Christian Fellowship/USA

"Evangelism can be risky for graduate students, possibly with career changing implications." Witness in the Academy is a must read for those hesitant to risk name and reputation in Academia. Mattson's book reminds us how "God goes before us" in this crazy, messed up world. While stressing that witness is discerning the leading of God, rather than technique, the stories and appendices in this little book equips the reader with practical tools for witness in the Academy.

　- Marcia J. Wang, Associate Director of GFM

"God goes before us! Could that really be true? If it is, it changes everything when it comes to our witness in the academy. I'm grateful for the ways I've seen God use Rick Mattson to encourage faculty and grad students as they consider witness on campus. More than that, I'm thankful for the gracious God who goes before us, and invites us to respond to his invitation as we pray and watch for his work in our friends and colleagues. This book will equip you to pray, listen, and talk about Jesus with freedom and joy.»

　- Melodie Marske, Regional Ministry Director of GFM

FOREWORD

THIS MANUSCRIPT HAS been in my heart and mind for 20 years, begging to be printed and published. Now it has life. As a traveling evangelist/apologist and evangelism trainer for InterVarsity, I can attest that every principle and suggestion in the book has been used and tested on campuses (and churches) around the country.

At last count, I'd worked in person at 80 different campuses. And in virtual space, many more. The list of campuses includes everything from local community colleges to Ivy League schools. And I enjoyed them all!

Names and places: Every story told in the book is true. I altered a few names and geographic references to protect the privacy of the persons described, and in a few cases combined two or more stories into one.

Hyperlinks: PDF copies of *Witness In The Academy* have clickable hyperlinks to resources. For readers of other formats, I've provided shortened URLs (when appropriate) in the footnotes and suggested google searches to access webpages more quickly.

Thank you to my colleagues in InterVarsity's Graduate and Faculty Ministries (GFM) for your partnership and your encouragement to write this book.

To the many students and faculty who participated in the evangelism training represented herein – thank you! You are the main reason we know the material is sound.

A hearty thanks to proofreaders Sarah Kane, Marcia Wang, and Sharon Mattson.

To outgoing Vice President of GFM, Bobby Gross: thanks for supporting this project.

And a special thanks to Steve Tamayo for help with production and marketing.

GFM: As mentioned above, this acronym stands for InterVarsity's Graduate and Faculty Ministries.

CONTENTS

LIST OF APPENDICIES

INTRODUCTION

HER AMERICAN NAME is Emily, a former PhD student in Mechanical Engineering (now graduated). When I met her, she said she wasn't interested in sharing Christ with her friends. We were sitting in the courtyard behind the student union at the University of Michigan on a soft September afternoon.

I said, "Could I serve as your spiritual coach for ten minutes?" She agreed. I asked very gently if maybe God was calling her to tell others about him. After all, someone must have once told her.

Emily replied with a cautious, "Maybe."

Three years later I got this note from her: "Many times in evangelism I have felt my lack of ability and regrets for how things could have gone better."

That note was written *after* Emily had led two of her friends to faith in Jesus.

What changed? How did the reluctant witness from a faraway country come to embrace the calling of evangelism at her campus?

After our convo in the courtyard, she began attending the outreach trainings we were offering. There she learned that God himself is the chief evangelist, and we are his junior partners. That concept alone seemed to make a difference for Emily. It removed the burden of initiating and "leading out" in witness, freeing her to a new kind of *following*. Or maybe I should say "fishing"? Either way, it was all in obedience to the one who said, "Come, follow me, and I will send you out to fish for people."

Fears and hesitations

UMich is just one of many stops around the country for me as I serve InterVarsity as an evangelist and trainer. In my travels, here's a sampling of the struggles I hear from grad students and faculty regarding evangelism:

External barriers

- Fear of offending (or losing!) a friend or colleague.
- Fear of being reprimanded, censored, or even dismissed from a faculty position or program of study.
- Fear of being seen as a colonialist, oppressor, or Christian nationalist.
- No time! Too busy. Long hours of class, teaching, research, and writing. Academia is very demanding. Lab culture is not always conducive to conversation.

Internal barriers (mindset)

- Belief that faith is a private matter. Whatever you believe is up to you. There are no consequences to our faith choices.
- "I'm an introvert." The prospect of more conversations and relationships is not appealing.
- Fear of imposing on others.

There's also the fear of not knowing what to say in an evangelistic conversation, or of hearing a question or objection to the faith you can't answer.

All these barriers are real. Yet, I believe there is hope: the hope of the gospel itself–of course!—but also the hope of being able to share the good news of Christ in a natural, integrated, unforced way. Hence the material in this book is crafted specifically for the academic world (but is transferable to other settings as well, such as the marketplace).

Who this book is for

Every Christian graduate student, whether in a master's, professional, PhD, or post-doc program of study, will benefit from reading the book and applying its principles.

Professors? Yes, welcome! One of my friends who teaches at a campus in the North went through the enclosed material, then recruited a dozen of her faculty colleagues to attend three hours of training to learn how to share their faith in their departments (I'm sure the free lunches we provided had nothing to do with their faithful attendance!).

InterVarsity Staff or other campus ministry staff, Christian Study Center staff, campus administrators and office staff: Hello! You are also "top-of-mind" for Witness in the Academy. I hope you'll read the book and pass it around to all the Christians you know on campus.

Timid in witness?

Whatever your position in the academy, you may think of yourself as being a bit timid in witness, perhaps wanting to display the love of Christ with your actions – but not words. This book is for you. I know you will be helped by the theology of evangelism laid out in Chapter 1 and the many suggestions for productive conversations given throughout the material.

And if you're a more experienced witness in the academy, the book will help you fine-tune your ministry while providing some new practical tools. One is the 3-Step Model of inviting to an event (see Appendix 5).

Structure of the book

Witness in the Academy is a short, simple book, written in two parts. The first part consists of a practical framework for evangelism in the grad world, sprinkled with many inspiring stories. Chapter 1 provides a theology of witness. Chapter 2 talks about discerning God's voice (spiritual research). Chapter 3 is about how to get into conversations and relationships in the first place, and Chapter 4 is about the various stages which people go through on their journey to faith.

The second part of the book is a series of appendices that provide practical tools for witness, such as how to witness both directly and indirectly (see Front Door–Side Door. Hint: start with the side door), how to tell your faith story, how to go deep in conversation, and how to use Scripture effectively.

I should also mention that the work will likely evolve. More appendices will be added in the future. That's the beauty of Print On Demand.

And I encourage you to read the book in community. Find a partner or two (or several) to share the reading experience, utilizing the discussion questions following each chapter. Witness is a team sport. Preparation for witness can be as well!

My Evangelism Profile

One of the tools I'm introducing here is the MEP: My Evangelism Profile. Inspired by the many personality profiles available these days, why not have one for witness?

The MEP is found in the 15th appendix. Its stated purpose is "to make evangelism easier and more natural for you by helping you identify your God-given design in witness." I strongly encourage you to take the MEP so you can thrive in the ministry of outreach in ways that are tailored to your strengths and interests.

Emily's closing word to me (and you)

Emily's note to me after she graduated closed with these words: "Thank you for always reminding me that God goes before us, and to listen to and rely on His Spirit."

That's exactly the idea here. Following God. Listening to the Holy Spirit. Sharing Jesus. It's the start of a spiritual adventure that happens to involve a lot of great fishing!

FOR REFLECTION AND DISCUSSION

1. What barriers do you find in your own life when it comes to witness?
2. Who shared the gospel with you on your journey toward Jesus?
3. Who on campus would you be most thrilled to see come to faith?

WITNESS IN THE ACADEMY

ACADEMY VERSION 2

CHAPTER 1

A THEOLOGY OF WITNESS

" **I**T WAS EVIDENT that the Holy Spirit worked overtime in R's life," reports Bok, an InterVarsity staff in the Midwest. R had shown up to weekly grad coffeehouse gatherings on campus and was interested in Christianity. Coming from a Hindu background, however, meant the transition to the Christian faith would not come easily.

But God had prepared R's heart. Despite some setbacks and the real possibility of resistance from family back in his home country, R moved forward in his faith quest. He read Scripture regularly and was active in a church. After three years of seeking after the God of the Bible, R made a life-changing announcement to Bok: "I want to make it official. I want to be baptized."

Shortly thereafter, as a public expression of his faith in Jesus Christ, R was baptized in the presence of his church family and friends.

God is active

The Bible has much to say about God's work in the lives of those who, like R, are seeking to find faith. Here is a sampling of passages (with emphases added):

- "And pray for us, too, that *God may open a door* for our message." (Colossians 4:3)
- "I planted the seed, Apollos water it, but *God has been making it grow.*" (1 Corinthians 3:6)
- "No one can come to me unless *the Father who sent me draws them.*" (John 6:44a)
- "*The Lord opened her [Lydia's] heart* to respond to Paul's message." (Acts 16:14)

In each passage, God is the active agent. God opens a door, causes a seed to grow, draws people to himself, and opens a woman's heart to the gospel. God is the one who goes out before us, who arrives on the scene first, who works in the lives of our nonChristian friends before we ever show up. Our job, then, is not so much to *bring* Jesus to people but to *discover* what God is already doing in their lives, then participate in his work. Hence Bok's observation, that the "Holy Spirit had worked" in R's heart before Bok had ever met him.

Based on the above passages and others we could mention, I'd like to suggest a "theology" of evangelism – that is, a summary of biblical teaching about witness, which can be stated quite simply: *God goes before us.*

So, if God goes before us, evangelism is first and foremost God's business. He's moving about campus, touching the hearts of those he's called to himself. And at some point, he draws us into the process. Notice the proper order, here. It begins with God, then we arrive on the scene. So, our first job is not necessarily to *proclaim* the gospel, but rather, to *discern* what God is already doing so that we can enter into his service.

In my travels to campuses around the country, I often hear students say, "People aren't open to Christianity on this campus." I reply with a question: "Are you saying God is not at work at your school?" This question tends to challenge the objection to evangelism that says everyone in a certain location is closed to the gospel.

Wherever the Holy Spirit is active (and I believe he is active universally), there is, in fact, the opportunity for witness.

Prof. Rick Richardson of Wheaton College offers a fine picture of this divine-human partnership: "We are junior partners in the Holy Spirit Detective Agency. We look for clues . . . [and ask], 'Where is God already at work?'"[1]

God the chief evangelist

Yes, God is the chief evangelist and we are his junior partners. This was exemplified in the life of a dancer named Maya. She was invited by a Christian student named Kayla to dance in her thesis performance. Maya mentioned she was curious about the Bible, which Kayla took to be a sign that God was drawing her to explore the Christian faith. This opened an ongoing conversation between the two dancers about Jesus and the Bible.

Often, God uses multiple touchpoints to plant a seed and open a closed heart. Li, an MBA student and former Buddhist, tells of an encounter with a man in Las Vegas several years ago. "A Korean man with a stall near my mother's boutique," as she puts it, gave her a book on how a Buddhist monk had converted to Christianity. Li read the book, which served as an initial encounter with God. Years later, Li and her mother were reflecting on the doctrine of karma

---

1   Rick Richardson, *Reimagining Evangelism* (InterVarsity Press, 2006), 37.

and how they must pay for all their bad deeds of the past. Then, an interruption in the conversation. A voice spoke to Li's heart: "You should become a Christian." Bewildered, she immediately shared the message with her mother. Both were clueless regarding the source of the message, but it spurred Li to begin attending church and reading the Bible with a roommate in Los Angeles. Li became a follower of Jesus and now looks back with gratitude at the various seeds of faith that had been planted in her life. Li had been prepared by God for church, Scripture – and salvation.

Again, that's our theology of evangelism. God goes before us. He's a missional God performing his work in the spiritual realm, calling people to himself. Thus, we are "fishers of people" because Jesus is already on the pond, fishing. He is angling, wooing, and gently pursuing. He is scattering seed, tending crop, and preparing for harvest. He creates space for us to operate, opens doors for us to enter, and tends the field while we ready ourselves for human witness – imperfect as it is. The Perfect invites the imperfect (us) to tell the story of the Perfect.

Of course, God could skip over us and accomplish the task of evangelism without our help. He could wave his wand and, by decree, force the world to fall down in obedience and worship at his feet. Instead, he invites flawed followers of Jesus–the likes of you and me–to accomplish his goals. And what could possibly give us more purpose and joy than to serve as God's junior associates in the Spirit-spreading, eternity-shaping, life-altering process of seeing our friends move, as the Scripture says, from darkness to light?

The bigger picture of the Bible

Zooming out a bit, we see that our theology of witness, "God goes before us," fits with God's pattern throughout Scripture of initiating things, of leading his people, of going on ahead. A few examples include

God initiating the act of creation (Genesis 1:1), calling Abraham to the "land I will show you" (Genesis 12:1), leading the Israelites in the wilderness with pillars of cloud and fire (Exodus 13:21), choosing Christ "before the foundation of the world" (1 Peter 1:20), and calling Mary to be the bearer of God's Son (Luke 1:31-35). None of these various parties chose God or went ahead of God, but all responded to God's initiative. In the New Testament, we read how Jesus bids his disciples, "Come, follow me" (Mark 1:7), and frames their ministry as flowing out from his own: "As the Father has sent me, I am sending you" (John 20:21).

So, when we stick to a theology of following God's lead into witness, we find ourselves avoiding the business of salesmanship or imposing our beliefs on others, and into the process of *discernment*.

Have you ever thought of evangelism as, first of all, *discernment*? Amelia, a professor in California, told me that when she learned of evangelism centered on the ideas of discernment, discovery, and detective work, everything turned around for her. She went from a timid if determined salesperson to a spiritual *researcher* – a vocation with which she was already familiar.

A case study: Ruth in 21C

As a speaker and trainer for InterVarsity's Graduate Faculty Ministries (GFM), I find myself frequently on airplanes as I travel to campuses around the country. One afternoon on a flight to St. Louis I sat near a young woman named Ruth. She was in seat 21C, I in 21A. 21B, between us, was empty. I asked if she lives in St. Louis. "I go to school there," she replied.

"Wash-U?"

"Yes, studying medicine."

"Wow, I could never do that. Must be hard."

"It's a challenge but I love it. And you?"

"College campus ministry. Headed to a conference in St. Louis. Ever heard of InterVarsity? There's a chapter at your school."

"Yeah, one of my friends goes to InterVarsity. What do you do there?"

Only sixty seconds gone, and I was fully engaged. The Lord had opened a door. Ruth was sharp and conversational. "We study the Bible and try to apply it to our lives. You ever read the Bible?"

"I'm Jewish, Reformed. Not really practicing Judaism. So, no."

I asked, "How do you define what it means to be Jewish? I'm told by my rabbi friend that it's an ongoing discussion in the Jewish community."

"True. Not everyone agrees on a definition. My parents are both Jewish, so I was born into it."

We talked a bit more about Jewish identity — Orthodox, Conservative, Reformed, secular. Something along those lines. Then she asked about my Christianity. "I'm an evangelical Christian," I replied.

"What does evangelical really mean?"

"Evangelicals believe in the authority of the Bible and all that it teaches about Christ and salvation."

"So, you take the Bible literally?"

This question comes up often in my travels. I was ready for her. "Just the literal parts," I said with a smile.

She laughed, but after a moment's pause turned serious. Looking me straight in the eye, she spoke abruptly, "Rick, am I going to hell? Please tell me. I want to know what you think. I won't be offended by what you say."

Whoa, maybe I was in over my head. I'd walked through an open door and, as it turned out, stepped into some deep waters. And maybe at this moment, I was sinking . . .

For the purpose of this chapter, let me suggest as a general principle that when the Holy Spirit creates a conversation, anything can happen.

There's no denying that God had gone ahead of me on the flight to St. Louis and had prepared Ruth–and me–for a lively encounter.

Following God is the key

Just to point out the obvious, it wasn't my cleverness or training as an evangelist that enabled this little dance with Ruth at 30,000 feet to take place. I'm not that smart, not that creative – nor do I want to be. I don't want to manipulate, sell, impose, or presume. *I only want to follow God into relationships and conversations.* That's it. And in higher education, where so much is on the line for Christian graduate students with their advisors, Principal Investigators, other professors, fellow students, colleagues at work . . . fear of evangelism can easily set in. If you're a graduate student, faculty, or staff, consider how you might follow God deeper into relationships and spiritual conversations, neither working ahead of the Holy Spirit nor falling behind. Only if you pause and pray and wait for his leading will you notice his footsteps out ahead of you. And only then, as you track with those footsteps, will effective witness take place.

But don't wait passively. Be active in your spiritual research. Exercise discernment in watching for a move of God in the life of the person near you who's not a believer. I'll talk more about the process of discernment in the next chapter.

Think of two names

For now, I'd like you to think of two people in your life that you believe God may be pursuing with his Spirit – pursuing them as only he can: dying for them, overcoming the grave for them, grieving at their lostness, beckoning them home to a Savior they don't yet know.

Identifying these two names is an imperfect art. But think: in whose life around you is God working? What are the signs? – curiosity?

pain? questioning? reading certain books? pursuing friendship with you? transparency about their struggles and concerns? asking or in some way talking about spirituality?

Write down the two names. And write down what you think God might be doing in their lives. Then start praying for wisdom and a chance to go deeper with them in relationship and conversation. Pray for an open door, just as Paul sought an open door through the prayers of the Colossian church, mentioned above. And pray for yourself – that you'll be prepared for anything, perhaps even something similar to the surprising and edgy meet-up I had with Ruth in 21C (the story of which continues in Chapter 2).

FOR REFLECTION AND DISCUSSION

1. Looking back to before you started following Jesus, where can you see God at work in your life?
2. What is it about Jesus you would most like your friends and colleagues on campus to know?
3. When have you experienced God's leadership or calling or direction in your life?
4. Who are two people the Lord might be inviting you to pray for in the next season of your life on campus?

CHAPTER 2

DISCERNING GOD'S VOICE IN WITNESS

N THE FIRST chapter we saw how the idea that "God goes before us" in witness changes everything. It changes evangelism from technique to discernment, from salesmanship to discipleship, from bringing to following. Indeed, we don't bring Jesus to people, we discover Jesus in people. Wherever we show up, we find that Jesus showed up first. We're simply responding to his call to "Come, follow me."

But if God goes before us, how do we know, exactly, where he's headed and what work he's doing? How can we discover and participate in the activity of the Holy Spirit among our unbelieving friends?

The answer, in a word, is *discernment*. We "discern" the presence and power of God in those around us. This process is imperfect and there are no guarantees we'll get it right every time. Yet, with practice—with both success and failure—our skills will improve. We'll get better at listening to the Holy Spirit and also listening to the people around us.

Imagine you walk into a lunchroom. One of your colleagues, Antonio, is telling two friends the story of his mother who's suffering from severe arthritis to the point of debilitation. As you listen you discover that Antonio's mother can no longer get around on her own, can't go to the grocery store or take out the garbage, can't take care of herself. She lives three states away and Antonio feels helpless.

Discernment notices pain. Discernment listens not only to the words spoken but to the heart and soul behind the words. Discernment, in this case, listens to the whole life of Antonio. Discernment prays for "ears to hear" the voice of God as he leads you into acts of service and spiritual conversation with your friend. Pain can be an open door for witness – not to manipulate or take undue advantage of suffering, but simply to follow God's lead.

If I were Antonio's friend, I'd get some alone time with him to hear the full story. I'd empathize and offer to pray. And I'd ask if I could help the situation more tangibly. Does he need to travel home for a week or two to care for his mom? Could I help pay for a plane ticket? Take him to the airport? And at some point, I'd ask Antonio if he ever prays to God, and, perhaps, if we could pray together right there in the moment. When, exactly, I would ask that last question – I don't know. This is discernment. It's art, intuition, following the Spirit. There's no strict formula.

Recently I was playing a round of golf with Nathan, an acquaintance I'd met a couple of times previously. As is my custom, I'd asked the Lord for a spiritual conversation, but I had no idea where to begin. I felt an odd prompt to talk about politics, a dangerous subject in the current heated political climate in the U.S. But instead of offering up my own political opinions (which I'm happy to do!), I simply asked Nathan to share his. Then I listened. I found out we have similar views, which indicated an opportunity to go deeper. Pretty soon we got on the topic of gender and sexuality, and then he mentioned, in passing, the word "God."

At this point, I was discerning the Holy Spirit at work. But in what way? I didn't know. So, I waited. A couple of holes later, Nathan complained of a severe sinus headache that was hampering his ability to hit the golf ball and even concentrate on conversation. Again, sensing an opening from the Lord, I said, "I'll pray for you right now." And I placed my hand on his shoulder and offered up a five-second prayer: "Lord, would you heal Nathan. Would you please take away this headache. Amen." Then I mentioned that my wife Sharon and I often pray for people's physical needs and have seen some amazing results (though not every time). I gave a couple of examples. Another two holes passed, and I checked in with Nathan again, mentioning that we needed to keep praying for his headache. He replied, "No need. It's completely gone." Wow, an act of God right on the spot. I'm glad I offered to pray in the first place.

Discernment comes through prayer and curiosity. I often pray, "God, would you please open doors of conversation today in this place?" This is an excellent (and somewhat scary) prayer to utter before the Lord. And when we land in people's lives, we learn of their possible openness to spiritual matters by asking questions. Thus: begin by asking questions on the surface and see where it goes. Does it lead to more meaningful topics, or does the dialogue stay on the surface? (With Nathan, there were a couple of quick questions about job and family before we landed on politics. The topic of politics didn't fly in from the clear blue.) And let me pause and remind us that *we're not trying to manipulate, calculate, or postulate!* We're not trying to maneuver people into position for witness. Rather, we're simply trying to *find God* in the lives of those around us, as we care for them. Nothing more than that! Finding God is our primary goal.

One test of the other person's openness to deeper issues is to share something deeper from *our* own life. Our transparency often evokes the same from them. But not always. Sometimes I find myself being a bit vulnerable with nothing reciprocated from the other person. Then I feel hung out to dry, but this is okay. As Christians, we don't need anyone's approval to be secure. Security is found in Christ. By establishing our identity firmly in his love we're in great position to take certain risks in conversation.

When surface questions do lead to more significant topics, it's a sign of openness, a sign that our dialogue partner is a "person of peace" who's willing to talk about spiritual subjects. Then we need more prayer to walk in lockstep with the Holy Spirit about how to proceed. We don't want to get ahead in our enthusiasm or fall behind in neglect. Just . . . keep . . . praying. And listening – listening to God and listening to the whole life of this fine person, made in the image of God, that the Lord has placed before us. Again, discernment is an art. There's no perfect way to do it. I wish I could claim 100% success in the craft of discernment. Alas, not even close. But when I do hear a divine prompt correctly and obey, vistas open before me, barriers fall away, and the world is suddenly enchanted. A new adventure of witness takes flight. And I find myself in a kind of heavenly glory, joyfully opening my heart to a fellow fallen soul and telling them the story of Jesus.

One of the grad students I work with in New Jersey, Peter, felt stymied in his conversations with a fellow runner named Trey. Things seemed to be going nowhere. Maybe God had not yet prepared Trey for a conversation? I suggested to Peter that he simply ask Trey if he was okay talking about religious topics. Peter made the ask, and Trey responded positively, propelling their dialogue forward. This is an example of asking a straightforward question that provides instant feedback from a nonChristian friend. Do they want to talk – yes or no? This approach takes the uncertainty out of the process of discernment. There's no need for discernment to be mystical and mysterious all the time. I love asking permission from my nonChristian friends to speak about a topic. I might say, "Hey can I ask you a personal question? Feel free to decline if you wish," (or, "Can I ask you a religious question?"), and nine times out of ten the person will grant permission. Now I have a platform on which to begin a conversation.

Four tests of whether God is leading

As we try to discern the leading of God, some time-tested practices can help us in every situation. In *Longing For Revival*, Choung and Pfeiffer write, "The more you get to know God, the more you'll recognize what he's trying to say to you." Here are four of their discernment questions, adapted slightly, for discovering God's leading:[2]

1. Is the leading biblical? If we seem to receive a prompt for witness but aren't sure if it's from the Lord, we can at least partially verify its source by its agreement (or not) with Scripture. A prompt to be rude or domineering or dishonest, for example, is not biblical, so not a genuine call from God – nor is any prompt that involves moral compromise. On the other hand, a prompt to love an enemy, even if uncomfortable for us, is quite likely a summons from God. And when a door for witness seems to open in places like restaurants, Uber cabs, and airplanes, there's certainly nothing in the Bible forbidding a small risk on our part to enter a spiritual conversation. Just think of Acts 8 where the Spirit guides Philip to board the chariot of a certain Ethiopian eunuch to share the gospel message. "Evangelism in moving vehicles" is certainly fair game in the Bible! One day on a shuttle ride to an airport in Florida I asked the driver a couple of innocent questions about his work and family, and he proceeded to tell me about his wife at home, pregnant, while he held down two jobs to pay bills. I said, "Karl, I don't know if you're a praying man, but could I pray for you right now?" When he agreed I added, "I'll close

---

2   James Choung and Ryan Pfeiffer, *Longing For Revival* (InterVarsity Press, 2020), 176-79.

my eyes and pray, but please keep yours open!" Then I prayed for him as he drove and gave him a $20 tip and a copy of *Faith Unexpected* when we reached our destination.[3]

2. What did you hear in prayer? This is the call to ask God directly for discernment and to spend time in quietude, listening for his voice. But even then, how can we distinguish God's voice from our own internal chatter? The key is to be so familiar with the Lord of Scripture that we can recognize his voice in any given situation. And it takes practice. Think of someone you know well, such as a parent or sibling or close friend. You have a good idea of what they would do or say in most circumstances because you know their character, manner, and voice. And that's how it is with God. Choung and Pfeifer remind us of Jesus' teaching in John 10:27, that the sheep respond to the shepherd because they "listen to my voice . . . and they follow me." Listen and follow. That's a perfect summary of the task of evangelism.

As we walk into our departments at school and into housing units, parties, airplanes, lunch meetings, outings—anywhere—we can ask the Lord for opportunities to join in the kingdom work he's already doing. We can ask for "eyes to see and ears to hear" divine activity in those around us. And when we get next to someone for a conversation we can ask the Lord, "What do you want me to say to this lovely person made in your image? Please give me supernatural insight into their life." Then simply watch for the Spirit's leading and dive in. I think you'll be amazed at the opportunities for witness that come your way.

3. What if fear wasn't involved?[4] Choung and Pfeiffer direct us to 1 John 4:18: "There is no fear in love. But perfect love drives out fear."

When we allow God's perfect love to drive fear from our hearts, we can enter the grad world with fresh confidence. Such confidence

---

3   https://faithunexpectedstories.com/

4   The call to not be afraid is found over 300 times in the Bible. And in 2 Timothy 1:7, Paul writes to his young protege, "For the Spirit God gave us does not make us timid, but gives us power, love and self-discipline."

doesn't arise from "self-empowerment" or internal assertions of "I'm amazing" – which are the vain assurances of pop culture (and sometimes academic culture). On the contrary, we find strength because the Lord is strong. We find confidence not by chasing confidence itself but by humbling ourselves before God. Confidence is a byproduct of humility and obedience. Evangelism can be risky for graduate students, possibly with career-changing implications. I'm not suggesting we take these risks lightly, but I'm suggesting they should not ultimately determine the course of our lives. If God is at work and we follow him into the fray, he will protect us, one way or another. Fear is not our master.

A classic example of obedient risk-taking is Daniel and his companions, exiled to Babylon in the 6th c. BC. Daniel places his devotion to God above the governing authority, King Nebuchadnezzar, upon risk of death. Daniel refuses to defile himself with the king's food, he ventures an interpretation of the king's mysterious dream, and he refuses to bow down to the king's idol (Daniel 1-3). The threat of being executed for each of these moves is very real for Daniel and his companions. As the story unfolds, we see that Daniel consistently acts with respect and prudence toward his captors, winning favor with the king and his servants.

I'd like to have been there at the moment Daniel's company first entered Babylon. I'd like to have asked Daniel the question Choung and Pfeiffer recommend: *"What would you do [here in Babylon] if fear was not involved?"* I assume Daniel's answer would be something like, "Live in obedience to the sovereign Lord whose power is much greater than the local sovereign king, Nebuchadnezzar." And who knows, maybe there was still some fear involved for Daniel. Yet, his fear, if present, did not control him, and isn't mentioned in the text. So if we remove fear from the equation–fear of rejection, fear of being awkward, fear of losing a friend–where does that leave us? If we eliminate fear as a factor, much of our confusion around evangelism is cleared away.

I remember playing a round of golf a few years ago with a powerful, intimidating man named Julian. He was a business owner with a prestigious graduate degree on his resume and was well known for a forceful personality made more volatile by alcohol abuse. Yet, Julian treated me with courtesy, overall; I never once suffered his wrath. On the ninth hole, I asked him bluntly (for he was a blunt man), "Sir, have you ever placed your faith in Jesus Christ as your Lord and Savior?" It had taken me eight holes of golf to work up to that critical moment, a gale-force wind of fear holding me back the entire way. But the instant I stepped out in faith and popped the question, all sense of dread in my spirit melted off, and I started thinking clearly. Julian the intimidating tycoon was suddenly mortal again, God was back on his throne, and I was in a zone of fearless obedience. Man could not harm me. But even if he did, so what? Better to please God in eternity than human authority on earth. The Scripture bids, "Do not be afraid of those who kill the body but cannot kill the soul" (Matt 10:28). Indeed, perfect love casts out fear.

4. Is the Christian community involved in your witness? I believe evangelism is essentially a communal affair, including the process of discernment. When we find ourselves in a rich communal environment of worship, prayer, Scripture, and the mutuality of speaking into each other's lives, God's will for everything—including witness—becomes much clearer. In the many evangelism cohorts of grad students and faculty that I've led (on Zoom), we reserve time at the end of meetings for personalized *coaching*. Working in pairs, each person coaches their partner for fifteen minutes, then the roles are reversed. The main coaching question is, "Would X work?" X represents a particular activity of witness, such as telling your faith story or sharing a gospel outline. The intent of the question goes deeper, however. It's meant to imply, "Is God opening a door for X?" That is, is God opening a door to share your faith story or gospel outline, or to invite your friend to a concert or lecture or Bible study, etc.? One evening on a cohort call I received coaching from Inis, a PhD chemistry student at Columbia University (NY). She asked me if it would work to text some Scripture verses to my friend, Richard. I hadn't thought of that idea per se, but when Inis suggested it, I recognized immediately that God had paved a way for it to happen. So, I texted a short passage from the book of Exodus to Richard; he responded well, and our conversation is currently ongoing. Coaching is just one example of a community-based discernment process for discovering God's activity in the lives of nonChristian friends. Another is to hold regular prayer meetings for evangelism. Specific names of nonChristian friends can be brought to the community, whose members can petition the Lord for a positive response. At one campus in the Midwest that I visited several times, we kept a spreadsheet of first names of nonChristian friends whom, we believed, God had placed on our hearts and in our lives. One or two of them eventually came to faith. Another method is used by the youth ministry at my church in Minnesota. They write the first names of nonChristian friends on ping-pong balls, which are held in a large glass container. Each week they pull out several balls and pray for the names (not really a grad world idea but take it to your church).

In summary, thinking of our part in evangelism as being, first of all, *discernment*, takes seriously our theology of evangelism discussed in chapter one – that God goes before us. God is the chief evangelist; we are the junior partners. Whatever initiative we take in witness is not a "first step" at all, but a response to God's invitation to follow him into the adventure of evangelism.

Returning to Ruth

Before this chapter closes, I had promised to relate the next part of my remarkable convo with Ruth in 21C on our plane flight to St. Louis. If you remember, her candid question to me after a few minutes of discussion was, "Rick, am I going to hell? Please tell me. I want to know what you think. I won't be offended by what you say."

When Ruth asked that question, I hesitated. But she reassured me: "Seriously. I want to know."

Looking back across the empty seat between us, I could no longer see Ruth's face. Just her profile in the fading 6pm light, framed in the cabin window at 30,000 feet. "Hell is a place God will never bother you again," I said. "None of his good gifts will be there. Is that what you want? It's your choice."

"I believe even an atheist will be accepted by God if they're a good person. More so than a bad religious person," she asserted.

"May I challenge you with something?" I asked.

"Sure."

"It sounds like you're saying that anyone who's a good person will be accepted by God. It doesn't really depend on any religious commitments."

"Right."

"That goes against what Jesus claimed. He said the only pathway to God is through him. It sounds like you're saying Jesus was mistaken."

"Yes . . . I suppose I am."

"If Jesus really is the Son of God, don't you think we're wise to listen to his teachings?"

"I hadn't thought of it that way."

"Never sit by an evangelist on an airplane," I grinned.

She laughed and waved a hand. "No, I love these conversations. I find them enlightening."

"You're a brave soul."

I asked about her studies. She feels called to be a doctor (like her father), to help people in need. She explained their affiliation with an organization that provides free medical services to the rural poor in Latin America. She was articulate and impressive.

God was with me. I suggested she think of her calling and abilities as divine gifts and that if she would connect them to Jesus, they'd come alive more than ever. She'd be empowered beyond her imaginings.

"I'll have to think about that," she reflected.

St. Louis was imminent. Before touchdown, our conversation took one more remarkable turn, which I'll share with you in the next chapter.

Debrief

During my interaction with Ruth, I was praying silently – listening in stereo, actually, with one ear tuned to Ruth, the other to the Holy Spirit. I seemed to get nudges from the Spirit to ask certain questions and take certain risks. The critical issue was, of course, *how far God had prepared Ruth.* That's how far I wanted to go in the dialogue. No further. But certainly, no less. Since most of us in the grad world are naturally cautious and respectful, we probably don't go far enough in many conversations. We're afraid of offending or losing a friendship. But the question persists: *How far has the Holy Spirit taken this person?* That's a much different question than how far we would go in our own abilities.

Think of the two people whose names you wrote down in chapter one. Ask God for discernment. What has he done in their lives? Is your witness keeping up with the Spirit's work?

FOR REFLECTION AND DISCUSSION

1. This chapter shares stories of various doors of opportunity for witness. See if you can come up with your own list. Bonus points if you hit a dozen.
2. When you think about sharing the gospel on campus, what fears come to mind?

3. What spiritual practices could sharpen your discernment around witnessing opportunities?
4. How is the Lord currently preparing you to serve as a witness?

CHAPTER 3

TAKE A RISK, CLIMB OUT OF THE BOAT

N THE FIRST two chapters we looked at two main subjects:
- A theology of witness: God goes before us.
- Discernment: Our first job in witness is to discover ("discern") what God is already doing in the lives of nonChristians in our networks.

The subject of this chapter is *risk*. It's about entering the fray and becoming an active participant in God's work. Once we discern God's activity in the life of a nonChristian friend, how do we get on board? How do we enter the fray? I'd like to suggest that our entry point into the flow of evangelism usually involves some little risk on our part, something socially unsafe. After all, spiritual conversations rarely land conveniently in our lap. A good metaphor for this risk is to "climb out of the boat" and walk on water toward Jesus. He is there beckoning us with outstretched arms. "Come to me, take my hand," he seems to say. And then we must walk by faith across the surface of the sea to join his ministry of sharing the gospel with others.

But if you're like me you have many reasons to decline such "H20-strolling," and thus remain safely and silently within the boat. Maybe you're fatigued from teaching and research. Maybe you're introverted (this is me) and your introversion is quietly protesting additional time with people – which always takes more energy. Fear of rejection can also lessen our motivation for witness. Who wants to be shunned by a friend? Or perhaps you feel unholy and disconnected from God, which casts doubt on your ability to share him with anyone. And sometimes it's as simple as preferring a good book, movie, or quiet convo with a Christian friend over potentially messy evangelistic activity.

You may have professional concerns as well, such as worst-case fears that "coming out" as a Christian might jeopardize relationships with colleagues and even derail your academic career.

Yet, if God is involved, there's no safer place in the world than out among the splashing waves, dancing with Jesus. Jeff Roesler, an engineering professor at the University of Illinois, climbed out of the boat courageously, trusting God to uphold him in witness at a professional conference he helped organize. The conference featured a leading expert in civil engineering, a Dr. Ortiz out of Central America. But even in making the invitation to Dr. Ortiz, Jeff was aware of a sad reality about his featured guest: Dr. Ortiz had been diagnosed with pancreatic cancer just a few months earlier.

As the conference unfolded, Jeff prayed for an open door for witness, trying to discern the leading of God. Nothing happened until a spontaneous "open mic" session on the final evening. A senior international design expert took the mic first and, among his other comments, thanked God for Dr. Ortiz and his many contributions to the field of civil engineering. When Jeff heard the word "God" from the expert's lips, his heart raced. This was, he believed, the divine signal for which he'd been waiting. So, he disembarked an invisible boat and ventured upon open water, eyes fixed on Jesus. He took a risk. Stepping onto the platform, he leaned into the microphone and, well . . . started praying. He prayed for the healing of Dr. Ortiz's cancer. Prayed in the name of Jesus in front of 150 professional peers at an academic conference.

As it turns out, the guest of honor went back to his country and began exploring the Christian faith – reading the Bible and seeking to find God. A few months later, he spoke with Jeff on the phone and said he was at peace. He knew his time was short, and he was ready to die, knowing he would be with Jesus. Two days later, his son texted Jeff with the news that his father had passed away.

The power of practice

Prof. Roesler's water-walking was pretty daring, in my view. I'm not sure I'd have gone so far as to invoke the healing power of Jesus at a professional gathering. But who knows, maybe in the heat of the moment I'd have done it. When one senses the Spirit's leading, anything is possible. But usually, we have to build up to a major step of faith by taking smaller, incremental steps along the way. And this brings up an important point: *practice builds confidence.* Not "self-confidence" per se, as if witness depended on our native abilities, but confidence in God and his leading. A now-graduated student I worked with at the Booth School of Business, Zach, observed to me recently, "The more I step out in faith, the more natural it feels. And the less I step out in faith, the harder it is to begin." Amen. That is so true. The first risk in witness is usually the hardest, the second risk not quite so hard, the third a bit easier, and so forth. The tenth time we decide to obey God and climb out of the boat, it feels much more natural. In fact, I believe we were born for this – born for sharing the Lord with others, so when we engage in witness, we're reclaiming our original purpose.

Secular social norms tell us that evangelism is awkward and taboo. But in the kingdom of God evangelism is, in fact, a social *norm*. It's what we do. It flows from our identity in Christ. In my interview with Prof. Roesler, he implied the same thing about his own identity: "Am I a professor who happens to be a Christian or a Christian who happens to be a professor?" he asked. I find this a very challenging question. Is our primary sense of self in our vocation, abilities – or in Christ? If in Christ, then we will do as he does, walk in his shoes, go where he leads (even out on the water). Jesus says, after all, "As the Father has sent me, I am sending you" (John 20:21). We walk, thus, in the path he has laid down.

A master's student at the University of Chicago, Briana Payton, decided to climb out of the boat in a public way. She started a YouTube channel that would proclaim her faith in Christ widely, thereby opening herself, potentially, to criticism from friends, acquaintances, and other students in her program at school. *Bri, Myself & God* was born, a series of short videos about Briana's relationship with Jesus that also gives neighborly advice from a Christian perspective.

Briana is a friend of mine. She will tell you that the most important thing to know about her is that she's a child of God. Everything else is of secondary importance. The Lord spoke to her in prayer about going public. She listened and obeyed. Her witness thus went out over the airwaves of YouTube, sparking conversations with nonChristian friends and providing spiritual wisdom for viewers' everyday problems.

The true you

The past few years I've had the opportunity to provide evangelism training to many graduate students and faculty around the country. They're all unique in their personalities, spiritual gifts, ethnicities, and fields of study. I want to say to each one, "*Be yourself.* Take the kind of risks in witness that fit with who you are." There's no need to put on an artificial self as you interact with unbelievers. Yet, it's good to push yourself by taking risks that feel natural but stretch you. Myself, I'm a social introvert: I like people but I need time alone to recharge before returning to people. What risks would a "social introvert" take? In my case, I tend to bring up religious topics early in relationships and early in conversations, even with strangers. And the more I practice these patterns, the easier they become.

If you'd like to learn more about your own God-given evangelism style(s), please take the "My Evangelism Profile" quiz in Appendix 15. You may be surprised at how freely witness can flow from your life just as it is. If you struggle with evangelism, you may be more of a natural at it than you think.

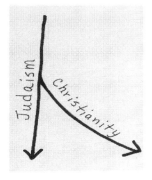

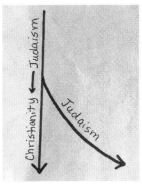

Ruth Part 3

I'd like to close this chapter on risk by relating the third and final portion of my conversation with Ruth in 21C.

"I have a diagram for you," I said to Ruth.

The light was dim in the cabin as the pilot announced our initial descent into St. Louis.

"Okay," Ruth nodded.

"Here's Judaism," I drew a vertical line in the air, top to bottom. "And here's an offshoot, Christianity." This is how we normally think about Judaism and Christianity.

"Right."

"But what if it's the other way around?" I continued to mime. "What if Christianity is the true Judaism and the offshoot is simply a holdover from Judaism of the past?"

Ruth regarded me for a moment without speaking. For the first time in an hour, I was aware of the low rumble of jet propulsion. Finally, I offered gently, "Am I pushing you too hard?"

"Not at all. I want to think about these matters. Maybe you should come and talk to students at Wash U sometime."

"Just invite me. I come cheap."

She smiled and we talked more about her campus.

The big Delta plane was barreling down through banks of dense clouds. Sensing the Spirit, I asked Ruth if I could put one final idea on the table. One I rarely use. She agreed without hesitation.

I said carefully, "Perhaps God placed me here to talk with you on this flight."

"You're actually the second InterVarsity person I talked with today," she responded.

I laughed. "Maybe the Lord is trying to get your attention. Anyway, I don't want to get a messiah complex here. I don't normally tell people that God placed me in their life."

"It's okay. I know what you're saying."

We deplaned and walked up the jet bridge together. In the terminal, there was a brief handshake as I gave her my card but didn't ask for her info. "Email me if you wish," I said lightly.

"Enjoy St. Louis."

It was over. I kept my distance as we wound through the terminal. *Lord, would you touch the heart of Ruth in 21C.*

Debrief

I took several risks with Ruth which I believe were warranted. And in this conversation, it seemed wise to ask Ruth's permission each time we moved forward to a new and more personal topic.

In higher education, we often talk about the value of "consent." Ruth gave her consent to an increasingly deep and more pointed dialogue throughout the flight. You may wish to try this: when a conversation becomes sticky, ask if the other person is doing okay. Or ask if you can bring up a new subject. Witness is, after all, a human endeavor. It should flow from our authentic selves. I never want to be *dualistic* – that is, artificially evangelistic. I never want to go from "normal" to "evangelistic" by temporarily putting on my evangelism hat (so to speak), just doing it as an activity, then going back to my regular self. Yes, there may be times when we are more intentional about witness. But in general, I want to "be" evangelism rather than just "do" evangelism.

One note of caution on this approach is to not retreat from witness by saying it never feels natural. Students have said to me, "I don't want to force anything. I will only do what's natural." So then they never take the kind of risks we're talking about in this chapter. My response is that *we don't always naturally feel natural*. We'll feel natural in witness when we connect our primary identity to Jesus and allow our lives to be a proclamation of his love.

One evening at Hamline University in St. Paul where I live, a new student visited our InterVarsity fellowship. When she introduced herself she moved quickly from hometown and major (as expected) to gender, preferred pronouns, ethnicity, and political perspective. Such extensive disclosure took me by surprise. In any case, she was proud of her identity and shared it without hesitation or embarrassment.

As Christians, can we do the same? It may require risk. But remember: climbing out of the boat and walking on water with Jesus gets easier and more natural each succeeding time we do it. And this fits with our theology of witness: Jesus is already out there, working in the lives of our nonChristian friends. Exiting the boat means entering a ministry prepared by God. This is a reasonable risk.

Back to your two nonChristian friends from chapter 1: What's a reasonable (and maybe stretching) risk to take with them next? What must you do to climb out of the boat and walk on water?

FOR REFLECTION AND DISCUSSION

1. Where have you taken risks in your academic career? What did you learn about yourself from those risks?
2. What do your friends and colleagues on campus already know about your faith?
3. Rick said to Ruth in 21C, "Perhaps God placed me here." What would be different about your time on campus if you believed more firmly that "God placed you here"?
4. What reasonable risk might the Lord be calling you to as you seek to follow him in witness?

CHAPTER 4

THE FIVE THRESHOLDS
OF CONVERSION

T HUS FAR WE'VE looked at three topics:

- God goes before us (chapter 1).
- Our job is to discern his work (chapter 2).
- Our next job is to climb out of the boat and participate in God's work (take a risk, chapter 3).

Notice the tight logic of the above concepts. God arrives at the place of ministry first, we discern his work in that place (in a person's life, for example), and then we dive in. The order is very important. If we take seriously a *theology* of witness, then God and his initiative will be front and center, and we can enter relationships with Spirit-led confidence.

The question of this chapter is: When we *do* enter relationships and participate in God's work of witness, what will we find? What sort of process will our nonChristian friends be going through? In

I Once Was Lost, Schaupp and Everts tell us that people tend to go through five stages in coming to faith, what the authors call crossing five "thresholds."[5]

The overall concept is that conversion usually takes place *gradually*. It's rare (though not impossible) for someone to go from spiritual disinterest or skepticism to a full embrace of the Christian faith all at once. People don't usually "leap up a whole flight of stairs" in changing their worldview. It's more realistic and more common that they ascend the staircase of faith one step at a time. And along the way, there may be landings – places where people pause for a while or even stop permanently as they ponder the call to faith.

I will summarize the Five Thresholds (5Ts, from hereon) in the present chapter. For a full description, I recommend *I Once Was Lost*, which in my view is quite a profound book.

Threshold 1	Trust
Threshold 2	Curious
Threshold 3	Open
Threshold 4	Seeking
Threshold 5	Following

---

5   Don Everts and Doug Schaupp, *I Once Was Lost* (InterVarsity Press, 2008).

Threshold 1: Trust a Christian (moving from distrust to trust)

Rosaria Champagne Butterfield was a self-described "leftist lesbian" professor of English. Disgusted by Christians in her classes and in the media, she wrote an article for her local newspaper which attacked the "unholy trinity of Jesus, Republican politics, and patriarchy." The article generated many responses, both for and against her position. One response particularly caught her attention – a kindly letter from a local pastor which, as it turned out, started a friendship. A very unlikely friendship. For Rosaria, Pastor Ken Smith represented the enemy, someone she would normally reject out of hand – but, in this case, could not. "Ken and his wife, Floy, and I became friends. They entered my world. They met my friends . . . "

Trust. It can be hard to establish and is very easy to break. Most people who come to faith start their journey by trusting a Christian. That's their first step. And that's what happened to Rosaria when Ken and Floy took a genuine interest in her life.

Jesus was a trust builder. A good example of Jesus bonding with a new friend is his encounter with a Samaritan woman recorded in John 4. She is hurting and seems to have low expectations of the Galilean traveler seated at her local well. When he asks her for a drink of well water, she protests, "You are a Jew and I am a Samaritan woman . . . How can you ask me for a drink?" She seems wary. Tension is in the air. The text tells us that "Jews do not associate with Samaritans," and "the disciples were surprised to find him talking with a woman."

Yet the conversation proceeds back and forth. It starts with a topic on the surface–cold water from a well–and continues to something deeper – the painful history of the woman's relationships with men. She's been rejected by five husbands. Perhaps she thinks this rabbi character will do the same. Perhaps he'll just grab his precious water and toss her aside. Instead, Jesus offers the opposite, something for the woman's healing, for the mending of her soul: *living water*. It will quench her soul thirst forever. She is drawn in. "Sir, give me this water so that I won't get thirsty," she pleads. She learns to trust Jesus in this conversation, to the point of spreading the word about him to all the local townspeople.

Myself, I'm not always open to reaching across cultural and social barriers to befriend a Rosaria or a Samaritan woman. I'm not sure I want new nonChristian friends (or maybe I just want them completely on my terms, without entanglements and obligations). Similarly, it seems many of the graduate students I work with are introverted, so it can be hard for them to initiate new friendships. Friendship takes energy, a finite commodity amid a PhD or master's program. Who has time for new friends? Who wants to open themselves to inconvenience and time-consuming conversation?

But if God is orchestrating a friendship, we need to jump in, you and I. God will give us the required patience and energy. He'll bless us in unexpected ways. We'll become more complete, more whole, more holy when we say yes to God's bidding, when we open ourselves to a "Samaritan" in our department or club or housing unit. Recently I took on someone at my golf course that I never expected to befriend. Too much of a burden, I thought. But now I find myself *blessed by him* in this friendship. Yes, totally unexpected, and that's how God often works.

Back to John 4, it was totally unexpected on the part of a hurting woman in Samaria to receive friendship—and much more—from a traveling Jewish teacher.

Three suggestions for T1, building trust

1. **Take initiative**. Sometimes the first step is the hardest. I find that opening my mouth and asking a question, such as "How are your studies?" or "How is your family?" or

"Do you feel like you're under a lot of pressure at school these days?" – moves the relationship forward. It's nice when others initiate with us. But usually, we are the hosts and must initiate. We belong to Christ, so we are bidding others, "Come and see" (John 1:46). That is the essence of our invitation to the world.

2. **Identify yourself as a Christian.** I have a habit of identifying myself as a believer early in a relationship. This is best done by mentioning in passing that I go to church or grew up Christian or that I'm praying about things. Once I've said something Christian, the table is set. Everything I do and say going forward can be interpreted by a friend as living out my Christian life. Sometimes this practice has hilarious results. As a golfer, it may come out on the seventh hole, for example, that I'm a man of faith. Then the apologies begin from the other person: "Oh, I'm so sorry for my language," etc. At this point, I can live "curiously" by accepting them for who they are and not expecting them to conform to my behavioral standards. I'll say, "It's okay. Just be yourself and relax." And if there is room for a touch of humor, I'll add, "Don't worry about me. The Lord is the one who's watching!" – with a smile, of course.

3. **Bond.** Bonding can't be forced. And it takes time! Maybe more time than we have available. But if we think strategically about how we spend our time, we can include others in what we're already doing. This is obvious at school and work, where we're automatically in the company of colleagues, fellow students, and teachers. But think also of meals, walks, hikes, bike rides, grocery store visits, concerts, lectures, road trips. These activities are perfect opportunities to invite along a friend who doesn't yet follow Jesus and bond with them.

What my T1 nonChristian friend needs in this friendship: They need to know that I genuinely care about them. They are not simply one of my projects.

A prayer for T1: "God, soften my heart for new friendships, for building trust with others. Hang a "Welcome" sign on the door of my life. Intervene in the hearts of my friends. Grant opportunities for me to be involved in their lives."

Threshold 2: Curious (moving from indifferent to curious)

Many people around us walk through life "head-down" and are totally into their own thing. They're not curious about how other people see and experience the world. They're not curious about Jesus or spiritual things in general. They don't seem to care how the world works – only how it works for them. These folks are stuck in T1 or haven't come to trust a Christian at all.

But when a person starts to show interest in other viewpoints or is asking bigger questions of life, or perhaps is sharing their pain with us, they are likely crossing the first threshold toward T2: becoming curious.

At this point, our calling as Christians is to *live curiously* (provocatively). That is, to talk and act in such a way that is intriguing to our friends. Many are watching us more carefully than we think. My wife Sharon and I were dining in a restaurant one night, and one of my acquaintances and his wife were seated a few tables over. After dinner, he mentioned they'd been watching us! I had no idea. After forty years Sharon and I are still pretty cozy together, a fact noticed by our observers. And they know we are Christians.

May I suggest: *Living curiously evokes curiosity in others.*

Living curiously is a way to defy false expectations of what a Christian is. Francis of Assisi (13th c., Italy) excelled at such living.

He rejected the prosperity available to him from his family and deliberately chose a pathway of poverty and service. Honestly, that's a bit radical for me. Yet the lesson is clear: whatever negative stereotypes or sheer ignorance people may have of Christians, we can cut across it all with our humble manner, actions, and words. In the case of Francis, thousands were so interested in his brand of curious living that they joined his community. And of course, they all knew he was a devoted Christ-follower.

Think of your reputation. How would others describe you? As a nice person? Christians can be nice people but not stand out from the crowd. Many nice people around campus are not Christians. How are we different? How can we evoke curiosity in others? Like Francis, we can show genuine care *in conjunction with faith practices.* Thus, we model care from a specific spiritual "location" of biblical faith. When we serve people "in the name of Christ" – that is, through service empowered by the Spirit, others will know it. This is different than secular caregiving. And if God opens the hearts of those we serve, they will become curious about the spiritual basis from which we operate.

Three suggestions for T2: Helping nonChristians "become curious"

1. **Be transparent.** Share about your life. Be open about prayer, church, Scripture, and all things spiritual. Talk about how you are experiencing God. Model generosity and humility.

2. **Connect practice to faith.** When you practice caregiving and service, allow it to flow naturally from your faith commitments. Jesus said, "Whatever you did for one of the least of these brothers and sisters of mine, you did for me" (Matthew 25:40b). Thus, when we serve others, we serve Christ. Additionally, I'm suggesting we take the further step

of disclosing to those we serve that we are Christians. My church recently did a service event to provide clean water for those in need. We wore t-shirts spelling out who we are as a church, which elicited many questions from observers. They knew we were practicing faith tangibly. And of course, we can invite our nonChristian friends along on these service projects. Often, they begin to wonder about faith when serving alongside people of faith. When you walk in Jesus' shoes (of serving others), you find yourself getting interested in who Jesus is.

3. **Ask questions, and listen well.** People in the global West aren't accustomed to skilled listeners. I was in a bar recently and a guy asked me a question. As I started to answer, his eyes drifted to the TV above my head. Okay, maybe I'm just boring? Or maybe he was simply as self-absorbed and distracted as most people in our culture. On the other hand, a friend accompanied me to a talk I gave at a nearby campus. Afterward, he asked several engaging questions that drew me out in a wonderful way. I felt cared for and listened to. How unusual. NonChristians who are becoming curious will become even more curious about spiritual matters, and maybe about Jesus himself, when Christians take the time to ask good questions and listen well. For further suggestions See Appendix 2: The 40-60 Model.

What my T2 nonChristian friend needs: My friend needs to see real Christianity in my life — a Christianity that challenges his or her stereotypes of Christians.

A prayer for T2: "God, help me to live curiously in such a way as to evoke curiosity in others. And may their curiosity move past me to focus on you and your love for them."

Threshold 3: Change (becoming open to change)

The jump from T2 "curious" to T3 "open to change" is usually the most difficult part of the faith journey. Think about it: just because you're curious about something doesn't mean you'll allow it to change your life. I have a strong curiosity about Islam, for example. I hang out with Muslims and appear with them on stage in panels and debates. I have a great love and respect for Islam. But that doesn't mean I'm open to becoming a Muslim.

Even when someone *appears* to be open to change, it may not be the case. InterVarsity staff member Jeff Barneson offers a case in point. "Some years ago, my wife and I invited our friend W to read the Bible with us. We would meet on Saturdays, make breakfast and drink coffee while we read the Gospel of Matthew. W and my wife had been friends for years—having met in their doctoral cohort at graduate school—and we made easy progress together reading about Jesus. We had great conversations and W was attentive to the text. She shared great insight and intriguing questions each time we read.

"After we finished Matthew, we went on to read Mark and enjoyed the same engaging conversation. But along the way my wife and I noticed something. Anytime the text suggested an interpretation or application that might invite W to rethink her worldview or consider a different relationship with God (Jesus in particular), she would divert the conversation to a technical point. Gradually it became clear to us that, while W trusted us and was curious about the story of God and Jesus, she was not open to change – at least not at that time.

"So, we prayed for her. We went on to read through Luke and John and eventually Romans and Ephesians. We see W occasionally — whenever she comes to town. She is still the same engaging person with a sharp mind and lots of questions—but as far as we know—she is not open to change."

Overcoming hurdles: Despite the hurdles standing between T2 and T3, and despite the many instances we experience of people getting stuck in T2, as in W above, progress is still possible. People do move into and through T3. They are open to change because God removed a hurdle. Recently I talked with a friend who wants to re-engage his faith which had waned over the past few years. He told of how he misses the church and Christian community. He is open to a new way of life, so our conversation focused on how he might activate his faith and connect with a church. I didn't talk him into any of this. But neither was I a passive onlooker. I tried to participate in what the Spirit was already doing.

And that brings us to an important point: T3 is probably the place we most need our theology of witness – that God goes before us. All the perfect evangelistic technique in the world won't, by itself, change a person's heart. Only God can do that. But again, *that doesn't mean we sit back and don't do anything.* After all, evangelism is a *partnership* between God (the senior partner) and us (his junior partners). It's through this partnership that barriers to change are broken down.

Going deeper with brave questions: At this point, I'd like to suggest a powerful way for us to contribute to this divine-human partnership, especially in the often-difficult process of our friends moving from T2 (curiosity) to T3 (openness): asking brave questions. Brave questions go beyond the usual safe questions we normally ask about work and studies, hobbies and movies, etc. Brave questions get personal and tend to be underutilized for fear of offending. That's why I sometimes ask permission to ask a penetrating question that hopefully will get the other person thinking toward new spiritual horizons. Here is a sample script I've used many times (assuming the other person's positive response):

Christian: It's been so nice to talk with you about spiritual matters of late. How is your journey going?

Friend: Going well. I seem to be learning so much.

C: Anything in particular that's caught your attention?

F: Yes, when someone mentioned X [let's say X in this illustration is "being honest with God"] the other day. I'd never heard that before.

C: Oh, is being honest with God something you've done in the past?

F: (a variety of responses)

C: Is it okay if I ask you more about that?

F: Go ahead.

C: Let's just say you were going to be bluntly honest with God right now. What would you say?

F: (a variety of responses)

C: Myself, I'm honest with God all the time! I do it in prayer. How would you feel about praying together for a moment – and you could be honest with God about your questions?

F: Right now? I've never done that before.

C: It's not hard. Just be yourself and speak in your normal voice. I can go first, and you can follow. Just tell God very honestly what's on your heart.

(pray together)

C: One of the best ways to connect with God is to read his word. Could I show you a place in the Bible where there's a very honest dialogue between Jesus and a spiritual seeker?

And the conversation continues from there, as the Christian opens the Bible to a favorite passage in the gospels where Jesus gets personal with someone. Or if Bible study isn't yet on the table, the Christian can continue with brave questions and prayer.

Notice that the Christian in the conversation isn't manipulating but is always testing the waters to see if God is in this encounter, to see if God is opening a door. Thus, the Christian is respectful, asks permission, takes risks – *risks that are in line with the Spirit's work.*

That's the key! Walk by faith. Listen in stereo, one ear tuned to the divine voice and the other to your friend. Ask brave questions of divine origin that flow not just *from* you, but *through* you.

Getting brave with you, the reader: I'd like to pause right now and ask you, the reader, a personal question. I sense the Spirit leading me to write this, here in my office. It's a brave question. I can't ask your permission to ask the question, but I'll take your reading of this chapter as permission granted. The question is, *Do you care enough about your T2 and T3 nonChristian friend to ask a brave question? To lovingly challenge?*

I recognize there are all sorts of complications in relationships. It's not always clear what we're supposed to say or do next. But asking a brave question can help launch a person from T2 to T3 – and beyond. A well-timed brave question could eventually help make heaven a more crowded place! We need to find ways to say to our nonChristian friends, What are you learning? How is God speaking to you? What's holding you back? You seem ready to move forward – could I help? You seem interested in spiritual things – could we read about the life of Jesus together? Are you open to Jesus? Are you avoiding him for some reason?

Jesus was the master of brave questions (or penetrating questions): *Who do you say that I am? Is it lawful to heal on the Sabbath? Why are you so afraid? Do you still have no faith? Why do you call me "Lord, Lord," and do not do what I say? But since you do not believe what Moses wrote, how are you going to believe what I say? Can any of you prove me guilty of sin?*

Speak the truth in love. Lovingly challenge your friends. This is *especially* the case for friends stuck in T2 who may be moving toward (and through) T3 – open to change. Anyone open to change realizes they need something different in their life. What the "different" thing is, they may not know. But at least they're open to new possibilities. And the Lord may just use us to prompt them forward, toward himself.

That means, for our part, climbing out of the boat and walking on water to ask a brave question that, frankly, may be as difficult for us as it is for them.

So, I return to my brave question to you, and turn it on myself as well: *Do we care enough to be brave?*

This question presses us to consider whether we actually believe in the exclusive claims of Jesus Christ and the power of the gospel. And it presses us to ask what distractions we have in our heart (and schedule) that may detract us from courageous witness. My passionate longing is to make heaven a more crowded place. Are you with me?

Three suggestions for T3: Helping nonChristians become "open to change"

1. **Roleplay brave questions.** Roleplaying may seem artificial at first, but in all the grad/faculty evangelism cohorts I've led, we've used roleplaying as an effective training tool. I think you'll find that the more you engage in roleplaying brave questions, the more naturally they'll roll off your tongue. This will serve as excellent preparation for following Jesus' example of asking brave (penetrating) questions of your nonChristian friends in the real world.

2. **Invite to read the Bible.** I like to start with the gospel of Mark or well-known passages such as John 3 or the Lord's prayer. But you can start anywhere in the Bible. To comfort a friend who's discouraged, for example, you can read Psalm 23 together. See Appendix 6 for a list of passages to use in a variety of situations. Our friends need to know that the Bible addresses their felt needs and concerns. And we're promised that "The word of God is alive and active. Sharper than any double-edged sword,

it penetrates even to dividing soul and spirit, joints, and marrow; it judges the thoughts and attitudes of the heart" (Hebrews 4:12). A grad student I worked with in Chicago shared a scripture with a friend during Holy week, and it sparked a conversation that led the friend back to a faith he had previously abandoned. In conducting interviews for this book, almost every story I heard of newfound faith involved a nonChristian's immersion in the Bible before conversion. God still speaks through his word. It's a powerful way in which he "goes before us."

3. **Invite to outreach events.** Sometimes a brave question is, "Would you like to join me for a special speaker at InterVarsity [or wherever] next week?" Outreach events expose our nonChristian friends to a variety of Christian voices that can speak into their lives. Evangelism involves teamwork! We never know which speaker, which unique voice, or which act of service God will use to touch a person moving into T3. That's why we need to involve them in Christian community and invite them to our events. For an effective way of making invitations that will greatly increase your chances of success, see Appendix 5, The 3-Step Method for Inviting to Events.

What my T3 nonChristian friend needs: A change in their worldview, including a fresh understanding of the real Jesus.

A prayer for T3: Ask God to work in the hearts of your emerging T3 friends in the same way he promised to work in ancient Israel: "I will give you a new heart and put a new spirit in you; I will remove from you your heart of stone and give you a heart of flesh. And I will put my Spirit in you and move you to follow my decrees and be careful to keep my laws." — Ezekiel 36:26-27

Threshold 4: Seeking (moving from meandering to seeking)

Seekers are usually easy to spot because they've moved through T3 (open to change) and are beginning to seek after a more focused spiritual life. Our job is to help them zero in on Jesus, and this is usually done best by inviting them to read Scripture with us.

"Connor on the coast" is a campus chaplain, and through an email inquiry, he met Xin, a PhD student and seeker of God. Xin was meandering between Christianity and other religions, so Connor decided the best course of action was to expose Xin directly to the word of God. They began in the Gospel of Mark, and as they read the text for several weeks Connor noticed a pattern. Each time a passage spoke of Jesus' authority, Xin bristled. He'd grown up under what he described as an authoritative government and was pursuing Christianity for its emphasis on free will. But when Jesus ordered the demons to come out or directed the disciples to obey a command, it was a sign to Xin that the idea of free will in Christianity is limited. The question then became, would God's authority be different than the authority of an oppressive regime? Or would God, too, be an oppressor? Would Xin be able to exercise his "free will" in the kingdom of God?

Discussions between Connor and Xin were further complicated by Xin's self-disclosure of being gay, and what the Bible would say about that. Connor needed to decide whether or not to keep the conversation going. He writes, "Xin seems earnest in wanting to be a committed Christian and also seems earnest in wanting to follow truth. It is for these reasons that I have continued to meet with him, even when he (regularly) rebuffs any truths that contradict his prior understanding of truth! My goal in weekly Bible Study is to let the text speak for itself and to show him places where he agrees. In those places where he disagrees, put the onus on himself as to why he is choosing to disagree with Jesus (or with the scriptures)."

Notice Connor's commitment to using Scripture. It's the best tool available to us in witness and the most obvious way in which God has "gone before us."[6] Notice also the complexity of Xin's story. It reminds me of how uncertain the process of evangelism usually is. I respect Connor for hanging in there and trusting in the power of the Bible to speak to a human heart.

God's word can also be heard audibly. Many times, the campus fellowships I've worked with around the country have brought non-Christian friends to meetings where Scripture is taught from the front. Whenever the privilege of speaking is mine, I center my message on biblical themes or a specific passage. On recent trips to the University of Montana, the College of Wooster (OH), and Ohio State, I taught about Jesus. The late author and apologist, James Sire, always insisted that *Jesus is the best apologetic for Christianity.* Everything we do and say in outreach must, eventually, one way or another, lead to Jesus. Jesus is the destination of all conversation, all service, all persuasion. He is the ultimate reason for faith.

Inviting our friends to places such as a church, InterVarsity, small group, Alpha, or Veritas Forum—wherever the word of God is shared audibly or in print—will expose them to the way, the truth, and the life. This is our job in T4: connecting a friend to Scripture – and therefore to Jesus, and let Jesus do his work.

Three suggestions for T4: Helping nonChristians become true seekers

1. **Invite them into Christian community.** There's a tradition in Irish Christianity that goes back to St. Patrick in the 5th century. Patrick was a slave in Ireland for six years and later returned to his former masters with the message of Christ.

---

6   See Appendix 6 for more suggestions on using the Bible in witness.

He formed teams of missionaries who established churches in Ireland, which later spawned monastic communities. These monasteries were not isolated and cloistered but were open to indigenous peoples – Celtic pagans. As the pagans joined in the everyday activities of Christian community, such as work, worship, and rest, they came to learn the ways of God and thus believe. It's as though they practiced their way into faith by adopting the rhythms and values of practicing Christians.7 On campus, in faculty and graduate fellowships, we have the opportunity to organize ourselves into similar "open" monastic communities that model work, rest, prayer, and study. In these activities, we display a compelling liturgy of life. Those who join us from secular or other religious/ spiritual backgrounds can learn the gospel firsthand. This model requires a degree of hospitality on our part, but also a genuine commitment to embody the kingdom of God with no shame or apology. Soon, visitors among us will become one of us. I saw the power of communal witness most visibly in my several visits to the Edge House at the University of Cincinnati, organized by GFM staff minister Jamie Noyd, where those without faith in Christ joined the gathering of the faithful on Tuesday evenings. The recipe was simple: hospitality + food + music + Scripture. A few times I gave the message from Scripture which, I trust, reached the ears of the unbelieving. They showed up because they were invited. They stayed because the community was attractive and hospitable, and embodied the beautiful Savior in their midst.

2. **Read Scripture with them.** In New York, a student named Chelsea moved into an MBA (business) house and built trust with her roommates and their extended MBA network.

---

7   George Hunter III, *The Celtic Way of Evangelism*, 2nd ed. (Abington Press, 2010). See esp. chapter 2.

Chelsea herself was not an MBA student but this slight outsider status didn't stop her from starting a Bible study in the MBA house. "I didn't always know what I was doing," Chelsea told me. "Everyone stopped in and brought their friends from business associations on campus. At least 11 different countries were represented." The student most open to change was Leah. God was moving in her heart. Chelsea merely opened the Scriptures each week and allowed God to do the talking. Leah was beyond curious. Faith in Jesus wasn't something theoretical to her anymore but became a personal reality. She had found her faith by reading the Bible. As mentioned above, opening the Bible for our friends is the near-universal way of helping them place their faith in Jesus.

3. **Make a call to faith.** This suggestion is relevant for both T4 and T5. At some point in a person's journey through the five thresholds, they're ready to become a follower of Jesus, ready to receive the gift of salvation. We must offer the opportunity regularly for them to say "yes" to Jesus. This can be done in church or on campus by an up-front speaker, or it can take place in a small group or by sitting alone with the person. If sitting alone, I like to share an outline of the gospel message, such as the Four Worlds (Big Story) or Bridge Diagram, and invite them to pray a prayer of faith. See Appendix 10 for ideas and suggestions. One time at a campus in South Dakota, a student I'll call Lydia said yes to Jesus while we were sitting in the student center. At the moment of her conversion, a sunbeam shot down through an overhead skylight onto our table. We were stunned! While I never expect such signs from God, I was reminded on that occasion that the Lord is present and watching – and that he had gone before me to open the heart of Lydia to the gospel message (see Acts 16:13-15 for the story of another Lydia whose heart was opened by God).

What my T4 nonChristian friend needs: Help in clarifying their quest and prioritizing their most pressing questions. What is their most honest question for Jesus?

A prayer for T4: "Lord, I pray with the apostle Paul in Colossians 4:3-4 that you would open a door for the message and that I may proclaim it clearly, as I should. And Lord, like Lydia in Acts 16:14, would you open the heart of _____ to respond to the message of the gospel. Amen."

Threshold 5: Becoming a follower of Jesus.

T5 is the culmination of God's work, our work, and the person's pathway through the thresholds. It's such a significant moment that Jesus declares, "There is rejoicing in the presence of the angels of God over one sinner who repents" (Luke 15:10). Imagine that – a party in heaven celebrating the birth of a new believer. InterVarsity staff minister Pete Williamson tells of Elliot from England who was accepted into Harvard's one-year Master of Law program and attended InterVarsity's welcome brunch in the fall. Elliot had grown up believing in a divine force in the universe but had been put off by negative messaging from the church. Nevertheless, God was preparing him for something more. He'd already advanced to T3 – open to change, and that's where an invitation to a staff-led Bible study took place. Pete told Elliot that this was an "exploratory Bible study," and that he should attend. It was the perfect next step for the man from England who, by November of that year, caused a celestial celebration by entering the kingdom of God.

Elliot met his future wife, a PhD student, at another InterVarsity event. Two years later the couple was back in Boston, asking how they could be a blessing to current students. They hosted a Bible study in their home where they met a law student, Daniel, from

Switzerland. Daniel was skeptical of the claims of Jesus and the resurrection but kept attending the study, and gradually opened himself to the Christian worldview. Similar to Elliot, he'd arrived stateside as a T2 or T3, and returned to his native country a man of faith, where he joined a church and was baptized (*choirs of angels rejoice again*).

Not to overdramatize, but if festivity breaks out in heaven over the salvation of a single lost soul, what does that suggest for our motives and desires as God's witnesses? I'm continually amazed at the lack of zeal shown by many Christians for the ministry of evangelism. Many will say that they witness through their actions, not their words. But is this adequate? No, it's not. The Bible teaches that "Everyone who calls on the name of the Lord will be saved . . . How can they call on the one they have not believed in? And how can they believe in the one of whom they have not heard? And how can they hear without someone preaching to them?" (Romans 10:13-14). Those are some convicting verses. They tell us that being an upright, good person is not enough. We must find ways to *verbalize* the gospel, whether we bring our unbelieving friends into contact with other Christian voices who share the gospel message or give voice to the message ourselves.

Either way, the main theme and responsibility for Christians in T3-T5 is to invite our unbelieving (and newly believing) friends to read the word of God with us. That's where the Spirit speaks most directly and clearly, bringing many to repentance. As stated earlier, almost every single conversion story I heard in conducting interviews for this book involved skeptics and seekers reading and hearing Scripture for themselves, often in extended fashion for months or even years. One Christian PhD student in statistics read through two entire gospels over two years with a friend from Italy before the Italian came to faith – a long journey that had taken her through all five thresholds.

Three suggestions for T5: Helping nonChristians become true seekers

1. **Invite to Bible study, church.** Melodie Marske, GFM Regional Director in the Midwest, is fond of saying, "We invite." What Melodie means is that inviting is part of our DNA in grad/faculty ministry. We invite donors to support the ministry, we invite students and faculty to consider positions of leadership in our fellowships, and we invite non-Christians to consider the story and claims of Jesus. In the case of nonChristians moving into and through T5, we invite new converts—and those on the way—to read Scripture and get involved in a church. For Christians, church is not optional. It's not a voluntary organization that we can join or opt out at will. Rather, it's the body of Christ, which is a true spiritual reality. InterVarsity is positioned as a missionary extension of the church. So, while it's wonderful for students and faculty to find their faith through a campus ministry such as ours, the church is their eventual destination, their true spiritual home. So, let's follow Melodie's advice and *invite*. Invite to read Scripture, invite to InterVarsity, invite to church.

2. **Disciple them.** When a friend comes to faith, a new journey begins – the journey of *followership*. For some folks moving through T5, there is a defined moment of conversion. They may have raised their hand during a call to faith at a meeting, for example. For others, the moment of conversion is unknown or ill-defined. Either way, we must continue to teach and mentor seekers and new converts in the rudiments of the faith, outlined in GFM's four ministry commitments: spiritual formation; community; evangelism and service; and integration of faith, learning, and practice.[8] Each of these

---

8   Explained at https://gfm.intervarsity.org/about-us/our-four-commitments (https://tinyurl.com/y7x79phb)

categories has massive depth so that the process of growing as a disciple lasts a lifetime, both for initial followers of Jesus and us.

3. **Teach them to share their faith.** New Christians can be the most effective evangelists because they're usually excited about their faith and still very active in nonChristian networks. Helping a new believer write out their faith story and learn an outline of the gospel to share with others is a great start. It's also a good idea to ask the person to share their testimony at a grad fellowship meeting, retreat, or church service, especially if they can invite their nonChristian friends to come and hear their faith story.

Staff minister Hon Eng at Columbia (NY) tells the story of Joy, an international PhD student who came to faith through reading the Bible with another student and Hon. Joy returned to her home country as a professor and led her husband to faith. But it didn't stop there. Now Joy and Hon have started a Bible study on Zoom for a colleague of Joy's, a professor who's struggled with health issues. One person comes to faith (Joy) and shares with two more, and so the pattern continues.

What my T5 friend really needs: To make a specific choice about following Jesus.

A prayer for T5: "Lord, we rejoice with the angels in heaven over a friend who was formerly lost but now is found! We give thanks that you've given the gift of faith to _____. Would you help our friend grow in love for you and your word, and would you provide opportunities for _____ to share you with others. Amen."

Lessons

One of the main lessons from the 5T framework is that most people who become Christians these days do so gradually, especially in the global West where cynicism toward Christianity is normal. What's abnormal and surprising to many nonChristians is a new and blossoming friendship with a real flesh-and-blood devotee of Jesus who embodies humility, service, and grace. This person (the likes of you and me) may overturn an unbeliever's preconception of Christian character and intellect, and propel them on a path through the remaining thresholds to the final destination, Jesus himself.

A second lesson is that the process of evangelism should be strategic in that we invite our nonChristian friends into events and social situations that match the threshold they're currently in. For example, I'd be unlikely to invite a person in T1 to a church service that featured worship and an altar call. But of course, that invitation would be appropriate as a person moves into and through T3–T5. Similarly, a friend in T4 should spend as much time as possible in Scripture and in Christian community, so my invitations would reflect those priorities.

Sometimes we speak of "thresholding" events such as large group meetings, outreach meetings, and retreats. I learned this language from National Evangelism Director Doug Schaupp in InterVarsity. Thresholding refers to intentionally designing the context and content of an event to match the threshold level (or range) of our intended audience. T1s and T2s who are unfamiliar with Christian practices and doctrine need thoughtful on-ramps to Scripture, church history, and Christian language when these are presented at events. This is just basic hospitality on our part, yet I'm often surprised at how little consideration is given to guests in our midst, especially those in T1 and T2. And if I may speak a gentle word of exhortation to

Americans in GFM: let's make sure we avoid or explain references to American pop culture, geography, and history in our meetings, so that international students who are present won't feel left out. I've made it a practice to explain, for example, where "Minnesota" is or who "Tom Brady" is, or what the "Great Depression" is when making such references in talks or conversation. *Let's make it as easy as possible for the nonChristian friends in our midst to take that next incremental step of faith, from T1 into eternity.*

FOR REFLECTION AND DISCUSSION

1. What do you find helpful about the five thresholds? What do you find confusing?
2. With which threshold are you most comfortable serving as a witness? Which threshold do you find most intimidating?
3. Pick two friends and try to identify where they might be in the thresholds. What one activity can you undertake this week to invite a friend to cross a threshold?

CONCLUSION

BACK IN MY college days in Minnesota, I joined InterVarsity and learned about a concept called "Be a friend, share your faith." I obeyed by befriending and sharing Christ with as many people as possible. Honestly, it wasn't pretty. I was preachy and a bit arrogant, definitely not the ideal friend. I had found "The Answer." Now everyone needed to hear it.

The result of this bumbling witness was that I teamed up with several friends who were also sharing the gospel message with others, and we saw about 20 students come to faith.

I'm so thankful God worked through me in those days, and yes – in spite of me. He was out ahead of anything I did, calling lost souls to himself. One evening I was "cruising Main" in my '67 Oldsmobile Cutlass, not looking for trouble, but instead, talking excitedly with my friend Kathe about our new-found faith in Jesus. Another friend, Lori, was in the backseat, listening intently.

Four decades later I visited Lori and her husband in Virginia. She told me a story that brought tears to my eyes. She'd come to faith during her college days by overhearing a conversation between two of her friends while cruising Main in a '67 Olds Cutlass.

I had no idea.

Lori's testimony reminds me of how God uses us when we simply make ourselves available to him and step out in faith. When we make evangelism a way of life. When we speak and act and love even before we have it all together, even when we are still flawed persons and flawed witnesses, which we will always be.

Summary

We began our study in Chapter 1 by affirming a theology of witness, namely, that God goes before us. He is the chief evangelist, and we are his junior partners. Second, our job is to discern God's leading, and third, to take a risk and climb out of the boat to participate in his work. Thus, we disavow stereotypical views of evangelism as selling religion or imposing our beliefs on others. We don't bring Jesus to people, we discover Jesus in people through prayer, curiosity, and by asking questions (spiritual research). Anyone in the faith can do this.

At some point in our discussions with nonChristian friends, we'll invite them to read Scripture with us. This can occur at any point in the Five Thresholds (see Chapter 4), but especially as our friends enter and pass through T3, open to change. Here is where fruit is often born, as the word of God, which is "living and active," penetrates the heart of unbelief.

As a faithful witness in the academy (and beyond), it's possible you won't even be aware of the fruit of your labors until decades later when a Lori-like friend informs you that you made an eternal difference in her life. In fact, you may never know what happened – not until, perhaps, you encounter your friend on the other side of this earthly existence, in the presence of glory.

LIST OF APPENDICIES

FRONT DOOR–SIDE DOOR

Direct and Indirect Witness

Definitions

Side Door witness is indirect and is mostly autobiographical. You tell about your experiences, your worldview, your church, your testimony, etc. You're simply being yourself. You use a lot of "I" statements. Many students, faculty, and staff in the grad world prefer starting with the side door.

Front Door witness is more direct. It tends to challenge the other person's beliefs. Now you're using "you" statements. You're questioning why they believe what they do, and you're suggesting alternatives.

Scriptural Examples

Side Door: In Acts 26:1-23, Paul tells the story of his conversion on the road to Damascus to King Agrippa and his sister Bernice. Paul relates how he severely persecuted Christians, how Christ appeared to him, and how his life changed after his conversion. Interestingly, inside this side door presentation, Paul throws in a front door question (a brave question) in v8: "Why should any of you consider it incredible that God raises the dead?" This question is clearly more direct and challenging than Paul's testimony of coming to faith. Nevertheless, most of this section of chapter 26 is side door material.

Front Door: Later in the same chapter, Paul moves to the front door.

V27: "King Agrippa, do you believe the prophets? I know you do."

V28: Then Agrippa said to Paul, "Do you think that in such a short time you can persuade me to be a Christian?"

V29: Paul replied, "Short time or long—I pray to God that not only you but all who are listening to me today may become what I am, except for these chains." Wow, that's pretty bold. Agrippa is the Roman-appointed king of Judea. As such, he holds Paul's life in his hands. Undaunted, Paul opens the front door by challenging Agrippa's beliefs.

Basic Toolbox of the Side Door

- Your testimony of coming to faith
- Recent stories/experiences with prayer, Scripture, church, healing, blessings received . . . even your own doubts and foibles before the Lord.
- Easy questions to ask a friend
  - Do you have a spiritual background? I'd love to hear about it.

- Do you ever pray or think about the afterlife (if there is one)?
- What has been your experience of the church and Christians in our culture?
- Could I share my spiritual story with you?

• Scripture
- You might say this to a friend: "I know you're going through hard times right now. I'll text you one of my favorite verses from the Bible that may give you comfort" (see Appendix 6 for ideas).
- Or this: "In my world of Christianity and the Bible, human beings have inherent dignity. Here's a Scripture that means a lot to me."
- Or this: "Have you watched The Chosen? It's a great storyline for the life of Jesus."

Basic Toolbox of the Front Door

• Transitional questions moving from Side Door to Front Door, in the form of, "I don't understand X, could you explain?"
- "One thing that I never understood about Islam is why the Quran is trustworthy. Could you explain that to me?"
- "If I were an atheist, I'd have trouble with ethics. There just doesn't seem to be any real foundation. How do atheists determine right and wrong?"
- "I always wanted to ask ex-Christians whether they've left 'Christianity' in general, or Jesus in particular. Isn't there a pretty big difference?"

• Apologetics: making a case for the Christian worldview. All the apologetic questions about God, the Bible, church history, criticism of other worldviews, etc., are fair game (see Appendix 9).

- Invitational questions (see Appendix 5 for more ideas)
  - "I'm starting a reading group in the Gospel of Mark. It goes for six weeks. Would you like to join?"
  - "A friend and I are attending a lecture on medical ethics next week. Would you like to join us?"
  - "Have you ever been to a true Easter service at a church? Ours is great! Would love to have you visit . . ."
  - "Our graduate Christian fellowship is stocking a food shelf on Saturday morning. Would you like to help out?"
- Direct questions (brave questions)
  - "Do you feel satisfied with your life and beliefs?"
  - "Have you ever considered turning to God for help? He is there waiting for you."
  - "I'm worried that if you continue along that path (of cheating or petty crime or drug abuse or isolation, etc.) you're going to crash. May I make a suggestion?"
  - "Have you ever heard a summary of God's story? I'd like to share it with you. It takes just a few minutes" (then share Four Worlds, Bridge, Four Laws, etc. See Appendix 10 for more help).

Real-life illustration of moving from Side Door to Front Door

Fahad is a Muslim leader in Houston and an acquaintance of mine. He's an excellent conversationalist and very respectful. One day at Rice University, he and I spent a couple of hours in the cafeteria sharing with each other about Christianity and Islam. This was all "side door" dialogue.

That evening in front of 50 Christian and Muslim students, the front door swung open. It started when Fahad asked me why an almighty God would need to become a man in order to forgive sins. This was an implicit critique of Christianity and an assertion that from the Muslim perspective, the one true God, Allah, had no need of manhood.

After explaining why God would send his Son to die for sins, I made my own critique of Islam in the form of a question to Fahad (in this case, about the prophet Muhammad). And so, our conversation continued back and forth, comparing and contrasting the two religions with intent to persuade. That's front-door traffic! And it's usually necessary at some point in a relationship, especially as a friend moves through thresholds 2 and 3.

THE 40-60 MODEL

Conversation Skills for Talking and Listening

Definition

"40-60" is a conversational model that attempts to proportion a conversation to 40% talking and 60% listening.

Why this is helpful in evangelism

It forces us to ask good questions and listen well.

It's also a way for us to discern how God is working in the life of the other person. If the person opens their life to topics below the surface, we can be relatively sure God is opening a door for deeper witness.

The model also asks us to share something of our own lives. We don't want to turn the conversation into an interrogation by asking too many questions. Healthy conversation is a mix of questions and sharing. And perhaps the other person may ask a few questions as well. This is great because it's an invitation for us to share about Christ in our lives.

Scriptural example

In the famous "road to Emmaus" passage in Luke 24:13-27, Jesus joins the company of two men along the road who are pondering the reports of Jesus' resurrection. The men are probably in what we call Threshold 4: true seekers of Jesus, but perhaps not yet full believers. They're still figuring it out.

Jesus enters the conversation by asking a simple question: "What are you discussing together as you walk along?"

They reply by referencing the extraordinary things that have happened recently in Jerusalem. Jesus then asks a second simple question: "What things?"

After the men provide a lengthy explanation about the events surrounding "Jesus of Nazareth," Jesus moves from asking questions to sharing what's on his own mind – the gospel message, which of course is about himself.

For our purposes, I find it instructive that Jesus asks questions before sharing the message. Perhaps he is discerning their level of spiritual openness? We can't be sure. But Jesus is famous for asking questions throughout his ministry. We would do well to emulate him.

Basic toolbox of the 40-60 model

- Begin with questions on the surface and show a genuine interest in the other person.
- Practice active listening by responding with attentive body language and by asking further questions. Silence is good,

but a blank stare on our part with no questions or comments doesn't tend to move the conversation forward.

- Listen in stereo: to the other person and the Holy Spirit at the same time. Ask God for spiritual discernment.
- Be sure to share something of your own life and experience. The conversation should be a two-way street. But in the 40-60 model, *we talk less than 50% of the time.* This can be hard for some talkative Christians, who tend to dominate a dialogue.
- Be flexible! The 40-60 model is a rule of thumb, but it doesn't always work out that way. That's okay! It may end up being 30-70 or 20-80, depending on how chatty the other person is. On rare occasions, things go drastically the other way, where a very shy and quiet friend almost forces you to do most of the talking. You can usually avoid this scenario, but not always. The main thing is to follow the Spirit's lead.
- Ask deeper, more penetrating questions as the conversation proceeds. Try to get past hobbies and work and pop culture, and into questions of more significance. Ask about goals and values and spirituality – and be sure to return the favor by disclosing something of these from your own life. See Appendix 3 for this "onion-skin" approach to witness. Here are examples of deeper questions that can be asked when the conversation is starting to move below the surface:
  - For a medical student or professor: What do you value most in your medical studies? Is it the science, the people, or the service to humankind? What really motivates you?
  - For engineering: What got you into the field of engineering? And what do you hope to accomplish in your field someday? Any big goals?
  - (Adjust for other disciplines)

True listening

Are you the sort of person to whom others pour out their life story? If so, you have a gift of active listening that draws people out. Many of our friends are unaccustomed to being heard at the heart level. In their noisy world, perhaps no one pays them much attention.

But maybe you don't see yourself as that trusted person with whom others share transparently. The 40-60 model can pave the way to deeper conversations and greater disclosure to you from nonChristian friends.

Our goal should be to make the other person feel like the most important soul in the universe for the next 45 minutes, or whatever time we have together.

Think of a time when someone was hanging on every word you spoke. You probably have to think pretty hard to come up with an example. Ours is not a culture that listens. But the gospel is counter-cultural. And the kingdom of God is a place where believers in Jesus take a keen and exacting interest in the lives of those around them. The 40-60 model is an excellent way to get started.

ONION SKIN EVANGELISM

Going Deeper in conversation

Definition

"Onion Skin" evangelism is an approach to conversation that attempts to peel away the layers of a person's life to discover what God might be doing at the core.

Why this is helpful in evangelism

The Spirit's most profound work usually takes place deep in the soul of a person, where their identity and innermost beliefs are rooted. Tapping into this place in a caring way provides an open door for witness.

Scriptural example

In the Gospels, Jesus tends to get to the central issues of a person's life pretty quickly. What we don't know, however, is what prior conversation, if any, led to these pointed moments.

In Mark 10:17-22, a wealthy man who's also quite religious asks Jesus a question: "What must I do to inherit eternal life?" No light matter! Yet, this question is actually fairly safe. Rabbis such as Jesus talked about religious matters all the time, so this was nothing unusual. And who knows, maybe the wealthy man opened the convo with something more on the surface like, "Master, how are your travels going?" Again, we don't know.

To the question of eternal life, Jesus gives a stock Jewish answer: keep the commandments. Then he names six of them. None of this fazes the wealthy man. He has kept the commandments all his life. The story up to this point is uncomplicated.

Then Jesus digs deep, speaking to the core identity of his visitor. Where will the man's true loyalties lie, with God or with money? That's the crucial issue. "One thing you lack," Jesus says. "Go, sell everything you have and give to the poor, and you will have treasure in heaven. Then come, follow me."

The man goes away sad, for he had great wealth.

A lesson for us to remember is that *Jesus still speaks to the core identity of those he's called to himself.* So, when we peel away the layers and get down to the foundation of a friend's life, we're actually participating in what God is already doing.

Outer layer	Small talk	Hobbies, work, vacation, weather
Middle layer	Opinions, values	Family, goals, politics, money
Inner layer	Beliefs, identity	Spiritual beliefs, insecurities, family secrets, emotional health, addictions

Layers of the onion skin[9]

- In the outer layer, just have fun. Talk about whatever. Enjoy your friend!
- In the middle layer, ask about their opinions and values, and be sure to disclose something of your own. Remember that your own transparency will often evoke the same from the other person
- In the inner layer, ask about their basic motivations and cherished beliefs. Topics here may get quite personal. Be respectful. Go as deep as the Spirit leads. At some point, consider sharing a simple gospel outline, such as the Four Circles or the Bridge. I sometimes ask, "Have you ever heard a short summary of the gospel message? Could I share one with you?"

9   Chart adapted from Rick Mattson, *Faith is Like Skydiving* (InterVarsity Press, 2014), 173.

Final suggestions. Always . . .

- Use humor! Don't take yourself too seriously.
- Be humble.
- Listen. Draw the other person out. Find out what they think.
- Watch for what the Holy Spirit is doing. Pray into the other person's life.
- Care. Watch and listen for pain, longings, desires, unfulfilled wishes, stress, grief, disappointment, depression.
- Share about yourself. Be an open person.

APPENDIX 4

TELLING YOUR STORY

Background

TESTIMONY HAS A rich history in the Bible and church. In John 4, a Samaritan woman tells her story to a whole village, which ignites a revival. In John 9, a man born blind keeps telling the story of how his sight was restored. Nearly four centuries later, St. Augustine wrote his *Confessions*, which tells the story of his conversion to Christ. In modern times, churches around the globe feature accounts of lives that have been transformed by the power of the gospel. Telling one's "testimony" is a powerful and time-honored tool for witness.

Method

Telling your story generally has three main parts:
- Before Christ: What your life was like before finding your faith.
- Conversion: How you came to faith.
- After Christ: What your life has been like after becoming a follower of Jesus.

A way to remember this: "BC" (before Christ), "C" (conversion), and AD (after Christ).[10]

For those who grew up in the faith and have believed in Jesus most of their lives, you can talk about
- Childhood faith: What your life was like as a young person.
- Struggles in the faith (if any), such as doubts, falling into sin, etc.
- Adult faith: What your life is like now as an adult believer.

Scriptural examples

In addition to the two passages mentioned above, in Acts 4:20 Peter and John declare to the Sanhedrin, "We cannot help speaking about what we have seen and heard." Their lives had been dramatically re-routed by Jesus, and they simply couldn't stop talking about it.

And in Acts 22:1-21, Paul shares with an angry mob the story of his conversion on the road to Damascus. His "before Christ" account is that he was zealous for the laws of Moses and a persecutor of Christians. His "conversion" account is that a bright light from heaven flashed around him, and Jesus spoke into his life. His "after

---

10 AD stands for Anno Domini, or "the year of our Lord." In history: after the time of Christ, as in "AD 2023."

Christ" account is that he was called to be baptized and to become an apostle of Jesus.

Three versions of your story

- **The one-minute version:** You should be able to tell your story in just a minute or two. With the short attention span of modern-day people, keeping things brief and crisp is a smart way to witness.
- **The five-minute version:** Now you can go into more detail. You can include a longer description of your life before Christ or your childhood faith and subsequent struggles. You can talk about your doubts and what factors finally pushed you over the line of commitment to Jesus.
- **The long version:** For an interested nonChristian friend who's a good listener, tell it all! Share all the puzzle pieces of struggle and doubt, and how they came together in your moment of conversion or your emergence into adult faith.

Practice telling your story

Practice is a must, especially the shorter versions of your story.. Practice the highlights. Don't go into extended detail off-topic. Don't get long-winded. Often, newbies at telling their testimony go way over time. They don't realize their two-minute story has gone on for 12 minutes!

Make sure you emphasize *what changed* in your life. For some Christians, it was a life of self-centeredness changed to a life focused on God and others. Many Christians can speak of the joy and purpose they found in Christ, or of moving past addictions and destructive behavior to a life of spiritual health and service. Still others may speak of new intellectual satisfaction, peace with God, etc.

So, for you, what changed?

Practice sharing your story back and forth with a Christian friend so that you've got it down cold. Then pray for opportunities to share your story in witness.

Final suggestions

When the time seems right, ask a nonChristian friend if you could share your story with them. And be willing to hear any spiritual experiences or stories they have as well.

Your life "After Christ": adopt a humble attitude and talk about how God has changed your life, but that you're still in process, still have a long way to go. We don't want to give the impression that we're now perfect.

Remember the power of story in our culture. Books, movies, podcasts, and social media are filled with stories. Stories are often more persuasive than arguments in bringing about change in people's lives. I wrote a book called *Faith Unexpected* that tells the stories of ten people who came to faith, unexpectedly so.11 I've given dozens of copies to nonChristian friends and acquaintances. Again, it's the impact of story, of changed lives.

11   faithunexpectedstories.com/

THE 3-STEP METHOD FOR INVITING TO EVENTS

O NE DAY I was on a phone call with Bryan Enderle, chemistry professor at UC Davis and an InterVarsity evangelism coach. We were talking about how to invite a friend to an event. I suggested that we first explain the event, then offer reasons why the friend should attend.

Dr. Enderle shook his head. I was close, but not quite right. He insisted, "No, the second part of the invitation needs to be *autobiographical*: we need to share why we ourselves are going to the event – what it means to us. That makes the invitation much more personal."

I never forgot that. So, start with the event, then why you're going, then make the invitation.

Step 1: The Event – what is it?

Simply tell about an upcoming event. Explain what it is, nothing more.
- "There's a Superbowl party next week". . .
- "There's a concert on campus Friday night". . .

- "There's a special speaker at InterVarsity next Thursday"...
- "My church is doing a service project Saturday morning"...

Step 2: Why I'm going

This is the autobiographical part. Tell why the event is important to you. Be honest. Maybe it's an event that intrigues you or that you just want to check out or that was meaningful to you in the past. *Just tell why you're going. Tell why it's meaningful to you.*

- "I'm going because last year I really loved this concert."
- "I'm going because I'm told she's a great speaker and I want to hear her in person."
- "I'm going because it fits with my research and I'm always looking for good sources."

Step 3: The Invitation: "We'd love to have you join us."

Notice how we're communicating value to the other person in this invitation. We're saying, "It would be great to spend time with you. You being there would elevate the experience." This is much different than saying, "Hey, if you want to go to the concert, let me know." That's a passive invitation and doesn't communicate value. Sometimes we're so afraid of being pushy that we forget to love. Love is active, love takes initiative, love values the other person. Love is expressive – hence, "I really hope you can make it," or "Love to have you with us," or, slightly softer: "Any chance you could join us?"

Pro Tips

- **Threesomes are great!** If possible, recruit another Christian or nonChristian friend to attend the event with you, someone you know will go. Let's call this Person A, and should be an easy ask for you. Then when you decide to ask Person B, you can share that you and A are already going to the event. You can say, "A and I would love to have you join us." Tagging along with two people might sound more appealing to B, and you're more likely to get a yes. Plus, B doesn't feel pressured to come along just to save you from going alone.

- **Catch a bite to eat.** Often, I'll plan to get coffee or a meal before or after the event. Make that part of the invitation.

- **Offer to pick up the person.** Sometimes it's appropriate to swing by and pick up the person in your car or bike, or walk over together or catch the bus, etc. The journey to and from the event can be a valuable time for talking, building trust, and explaining or debriefing the event.

- **Use the 3-Step Invitation widely.** It works for inviting people into bigger commitments beyond one-off events, such as taking a class together, doing a road trip, or reading the Bible.

- **But don't do this.** Don't start your invitation by asking, "Hey, what are you doing Saturday morning?" That's precisely the opposite of the 3-Step method. Don't start off with their schedule, *start by explaining the event*. Asking first about the person's schedule can come off a bit sneaky, as though you're about to trap them into a commitment. But starting with the event is more honest. You're being upfront about the exact nature of the commitment you're asking for. Thus, they have an easy way out if they're simply not interested. Then you can close by saying, "No problem, catch you later. Let's have coffee sometime" . . .

- **"No" isn't forever.** Those of us who do fundraising for a living know that when prospective donors decline to give, it doesn't mean they'll never give. A few months or a year later when their situation is different, they might reconsider. It's the same with our nonChristian friends. A different event or a change in their heart due to God's work might yield a "yes" from them in the future.

Practice

Roleplay the 3-Step invitation with a friend before using it in witness. Practice inviting your friend to a secular event on campus, then a religious event, then a Bible study. Getting comfortable with the 3-Step invitation will make it feel more natural in real life.

USING SCRIPTURE IN WITNESS

Main point

Scripture is our most powerful tool in witness. Most people who come to faith in Jesus these days do so through extended interaction with Scripture. Thus, *our job is to expose them to the word of God and let the text do its work.*

The power of Scripture

The Bible teaches us about itself. This might be called the "meta" level of Scripture. We learn, for example, that the word of God is the "sword of the Spirit," is "active and alive" and can penetrate a person's soul and spirit. Scripture is "God-breathed." It judges the attitudes of the heart and is useful for teaching and correction.[12] This is the transformative power of the Bible that can speak into the hearts and minds of our nonChristian friends.

A scriptural example of Bible study with a nonChristian

Perhaps the most obvious instance in the New Testament is Acts 8:26-39, where Philip helps an Ethiopian eunuch (a servant of the queen) find the fullness of his faith. It seems the Ethiopian was already in Threshold 4 – actively seeking. In the passage, he is reading the prophet Isaiah but doesn't understand the meaning. V35 says, "Then Philip began with that very passage of Scripture and told him the good news about Jesus."

We know that all Scripture points to Jesus. Philip was the willing messenger. The word of God performed its work, and the Ethiopian was baptized into the faith.

Methods of using Scripture

1. Traditional method: Probably the most effective way of witness is to simply sit down with a nonChristian friend on a regular basis, open the Bible together, and begin talking about the text. You can begin in the Gospel of Mark, or anywhere you choose. Maybe try a few Proverbs.

A student at Harvard was reading the Bible with her InterVarsity staff, and came to this passage in Mark 8:29: "Who do you say that I am?" Her answer was, "I'm not sure." That encounter with the text launched her into three additional years of Bible reading and

---

12   Ephesians 6:17; Hebrews 4:12; 2 Timothy 3:16-17.

contemplation, until finally, she announced, "I think I'm in. I want to get baptized." She'd been converted to Christ by the word of God.

2. Social media examples:

- One leader in Minnesota runs an ethnic-specific study on Sunday nights on Facebook, with 35 participants both in America and his home country in Africa.
- InterVarsity shares Scripture on Instagram regularly. And the Evangelism Department creates "Insta-proxes" such as the Self Care proxe that can be shared on Instagram.[13] These proxes are meant to be interactive and not merely static posts.
- Former staff York Moore teaches the Bible and presents the gospel on Tik Tok.
- University of Chicago alumna Briana Payton shares wisdom on YouTube (see her story in chapter 3) that flows from the Bible. Her channel is called Bri, Myself & God.[14]
- Even good old-fashioned email can work! I started a "Summer Breeze" email to friends at my golf course. It consisted of a short passage of Scripture, along with my comments, once per week for six weeks. 39 people signed up for it.

3. Meeting Felt Needs: Rachel is a PhD student at the University of Maryland, and is committed to an integrated approach to evangelism, where every part of her life is a witness to Christ. On occasion, she shares various scriptures with her nonChristian friends that meet their felt needs. One friend felt defeated by a relationship and was feeling worthless and hopeless. Rachel texted her some verses about God's unconditional love, which the friend greatly appreciated.

---

13 tinyurl.com/3myterps
14 www.youtube.com/c/BriMyselfandGod/videos (tinyurl.com/2p835uk5)

Below is a brief summary of scriptures you can use. Hopefully, this list will stimulate your creativity so that you can mine the Bible for relevant wisdom for any and all life situations.

You can send a nonChristian friend a link to a passage or print it out for them. Be sure and tell why a given passage is meaningful to you (step two in the 3-Step Method of inviting), and how it might help them.

- **Anxiety, insecurity, worry, hopelessness:** Psalm 23. This may be related to job, research, internship, a relationship, health concerns, etc. Note v3: He refreshes my soul. V4: in the darkest valley, "I will fear no evil." And then the glorious conclusion to follow. Truly a psalm of comfort and hope. (See also Philippians 4:6–8.)
- **Life is spinning out of control:** Proverbs 3:5-6. Helpful when things seem chaotic. You can share something from your own life, and why these verses speak to you.
- **Fear, need for protection:** Psalm 91
- **Guidance:** John 8:12
- **Ethical guidance, purpose in life:** Mark 12:28-31. See also Matthew 5-7 (Sermon on the Mount)
- **Wisdom:** James 1:5
- **Feeling empty, unsatisfied, meaningless:** John 4:7-14
- **Economic justice, religious hypocrisy:** John 2:13-17. Jesus shows himself angry at the merchants in the temple. (See also Matthew 23)
- **Going through hard times.** How God might help. How to pray: Romans 8:26-28
- **Learning how to pray:** Matthew 6:9-13
- **Forgiveness:** Colossians 3:13
- **Comfort for the hurting:** 2 Corinthians 1:3-5
- **Tired, burdened, worn out:** Matthew 11:28-30
- **The character of God:** Exodus 34:5-7

- **Who is Jesus?** Matthew 16:13-17
- **Building a solid foundation:** Matthew 7:24-27
- **Ask a friend which soil they identify with:** Mark 4:1-20

Another resource: various biblical topics with references are listed here: https://www.biblegateway.com/topics/

How to start a Bible study for nonChristians

- **Pray:** Ask the Lord who he wants you to invite. Pray for boldness for yourself and openness from those you ask. Make a list of prospects and pray over each name. Invite your church or campus fellowship to pray as well.
- **Invite:** See Appendix 5, The 3-Step Method for Inviting to Events. This method will lead to greater success in starting your study. As mentioned above, recently I started a summer Bible reading group at my golf club. I used the 3-Step invitation, and almost everyone said yes. Here was the key: *I made the easiest asks first.* That is, I asked friends I knew would say yes (which they did). Then when I got to the harder asks, I already had a group going, which made the invitation easier for me and more attractive to them. A kind of spiritual momentum was generated by the early "yes's," which carried over to those I was less sure of. So, consider forming a "starter group" with a friend or two, whether Christian or not, rather than just starting with yourself and a list of names. Then you can all be inviters.
- **Study together.** InterVarsity has many Bible study guides to use with nonChristians. Rather than listing them here, it's best to just google "InterVarsity GIGs (Groups Investigating God) or "InterVarsity investigative Bible studies." But this isn't just about Scripture, as central as that is. It's about building

an attractive community. Ask yourself, Why should my non-Christian friend(s) come back to this study week after week? What's in it for them? The answers are likely to be hospitality, friendship, food, and fun. Arrange an attractive meeting space. Make your friends feel valued. Use an icebreaker to help people know each other. Spend a little money on snacks or a meal. Prepare the text well so that it will speak clearly into the lives of those gathered.

Bubble tea Bible study

Student leader Jessica ran a Wednesday afternoon Bible study for her nonChristian friends at a bubble tea house in the Midwest. But it was more than a study. It was a *community* where everyone could be themselves and talk about whatever concerns they had.

One time I was invited to visit the group to talk about the Bible and field students' questions. Jessica was cautious and protective of her friends. She insisted on interviewing me before granting me access to the group. My respect for her soared through the roof when I was forced to meet this condition! She was committed to giving them a *great experience* each week. And yes, I passed the interview and soon afterward enjoyed a lively convo with Jessica's nonChristian friends. And I drank my first-ever cup of bubble tea.

APPENDIX 7

PRAYING THROUGH THE FIVE THRESHOLDS

Written Prayers for Each Stage on the Journey[15]

(See Chapter 4 for a fuller explanation of the Five Thresholds.)

Background

Evangelism without intercessory prayer is mechanistic, as if evangelism is something we control without God's help. Intercession without evangelism is unfaithful because we deny the role God has called each of us to play in making disciples of all nations.

---

15   Adapted from InterVarsity Evangelism Department (tinyurl.com/45cd7tac)

If you have friends and family you'd like to see become new believers, you can *add power to your witness by asking God to intervene.*

2+ Prayer Cards

The idea here is to focus on two people God has placed in your life. These are likely the people you identified in Chapter 1. Pray for them regularly and seek to witness. You can order 2+ prayer cards from InterVarsity.[16]

Those five thresholds again are . . .

Threshold 1	Trust
Threshold 2	Curious
Threshold 3	Open
Threshold 4	Seeking
Threshold 5	Following

Praying through the thresholds

Each of the 12 prayers below asks God to move in the life of the person you're praying for in a specific way. And each prayer closely

---

16   evangelism.intervarsity.org/resource/2-prayer-cards (tinyurl.com/55t4k4zp)

paraphrases a relevant Scripture passage. Just insert the person's name in the spaces provided and put your heart into each prayer.

Threshold 1 (trust)

1. God, help me build a caring relationship with _____. Help me become whatever kind of Christ-like servant _____ can identify with so that by all possible means he will be saved. (1 Corinthians 9:22)
2. God, send people into _____'s life to witness to her. Send more believers into _____'s life who will exemplify Christ and cause her to want to know Christ for herself. (Matthew 9:38)

Threshold 2 (curiosity)

3. God, bring me opportunities to witness to _____. Open doors for proclaiming the mystery of Christ to _____, given all our present circumstances. (Colossians 4:3)
4. God, enable me to speak your word to _____ with great boldness. (Acts 4:29)

Threshold 3 (open to change)

5. God, open _____ 's spiritual eyes. Break the blindness on _____'s mind caused by the god of this age. Help him see the light of the gospel of the glory of Christ, who is the image of God. (2 Corinthians 4:4)
6. God, help _____ realize her spiritual hunger and desire for change in her life. Break complacency in _____'s mind. Thank you that you are constantly at work. (John 4:15)

Threshold 4 (seeking)

7. God, make _____'s heart receptive to your Word. Like the seed that falls on good soil, give _____ a noble and good heart. Help him hear the word, retain it, and by persevering, produce a crop. (Luke 8:11-15)

8. God, give _____ ears to hear. Help _____ see with her eyes, hear with her ears, understand with her heart, and turn to you for healing. (Matthew 13:15)

9. God, set _____ free from spiritual captivity. Help me gently instruct _____ when he is in opposition to you, in the hope that you will grant him repentance leading him to a knowledge of the truth, and that he will come to his senses and escape from the trap of the devil. (2 Timothy 2:25-26)

Threshold 5 (following)

10. God, give _____ faith to believe. Help _____ make a radical life change before God and an equally radical trust in her Master, Jesus. (Acts 20:21)

11. God, give _____ the will to respond to you. Bring _____ to the point that he declares with his mouth, «Jesus is Lord,» and believes in his heart that God raised Jesus from the dead so that he will be saved. (Romans 10:9)

12. God, provide an opportunity to invite _____ into a relationship with you. You want your house full, so give me opportunity and boldness to invite _____ to come home to you. (Luke 14:23)

See also: Praying for Not-Yet Believers.[17]

---

17 https://evangelism.intervarsity.org/start-spiritual-conversations/ pray-not-yet-believers (tinyurl.com/45cd7tac)

CAMPUS EVANGELISM STRATEGY

A Macro Approach

Main Point

The main elements of an effective campus evangelism strategy are like puzzle pieces that fit together in a coherent whole. When a piece is missing, it affects the entire picture. But when the pieces are all in place, the result can resemble the community in Acts 2:47, where "the Lord added to their number daily those who were being saved."

Three essential elements

1. **Attractive community:** At Michigan State a few years ago, staff minister Ben Low told me his secret to the many conversions they were seeing in the chapter. In a word: *community.* The main factors were fun, food, service to others, Scripture, prayer, and an accepting environment. Anyone could join the community and feel welcome and valued.

2. **Spiritual conversations:** At South Dakota State University, I witnessed the power of multiple conversations taking place. It seemed students all over the InterVarsity fellowship were in convo with their nonChristian friends. This created tremendous momentum for evangelism.

3. **Events:**
   - **Fun/service events:** Little or no Christian content. Includes parties, outings, and community service opportunities. These are great entry ramps into the fellowship.
   - **Bridging events:** Christian content on topics of interest, but not a call to faith. These can include lectures, talks, panels, videos, debates, Bible studies, etc.
   - **Harvest events:** Includes a call to faith. This can take place at large group, small groups, retreats, conferences, one-to-one meetings, etc.

The coherence of the model

Note that every element is needed. Without attractive community, few will join our fellowship. Without spiritual conversations, we'll have no one to invite to events. Without events, we'll have nothing for nonChristians to attend (and without harvest events, we'll rarely if ever call people to faith, resulting in few if any conversions).

An example of a bridging event is a simple worship night held by a small group of medical students in Texas. Burdened for their fellow students, they emailed all 120 members of their class, inviting them to the event in a friend's backyard. But who would come to a worship night? "It was nerve-wracking," one leader said. "We thought, what if everyone thinks this is a dumb idea and just laughs at us? What if no one shows up?" But 25 did show up. They experienced live worship music (some even sang along), heard the gospel, and were given printed song lyrics and Bible verses to take home. In the days after, several students asked when the event would happen again.

One of the main benefits of events is that our friends are exposed to multiple Christian voices. Regarding the ministry in Corinth, the Apostle Paul observes, "I planted the seed, Apollos watered it, but God has been making it grow" (1 Corinthians 3:6-7a). Indeed, effective evangelism is often a matter of teamwork.

Contextualize!

Now that the model is presented, go ahead and change it for your context. Your campus may have a different way of doing things. Your group may be meeting off-campus or be centered around a monthly event or consist solely of a reading group. In any case, keep the main elements above in mind for the future, for a well-rounded ministry.

FOR REFLECTION AND DISCUSSION

1. What happens if one or more of the main elements is missing?
2. How is your chapter or group doing on each of the main elements: conversations, community, and events?
3. How can your chapter or group create its own events? Or use the events others are creating on or near campus?

4. Bridging events: How can you appeal to the intellect? Emotions? Spirit/soul?

5. When is the last time your chapter or group did a call to faith? When is the next one scheduled?

APOLOGETIC METHOD

Making a Case for Faith, Answering Hard Questions

Definition of apologetics

To defend or make a case for a position – in this case, Christian faith.

Scriptural examples

- 1 Peter 3:15b: "Always be prepared to give an answer to every-one who asks you to give the reason for the hope that you have. But do this with gentleness and respect."
- John 14:11: [Jesus said], "Believe me when I say that I am in the Father and the Father is in me; or at least believe on the evidence of the works themselves."

- Acts 19:8: "Paul entered the synagogue and spoke boldly there for three months, arguing persuasively about the kingdom of God."

Stump the Chump

My experience in serving as the chump in "Stump the Chump" (Q&A) sessions on campus, maybe 150 times, is that students have a ton of questions about Christian faith. So, apologetics is very relevant. And I've learned that my tone of voice and manner are just as important as the answers I give. Often, the "soft skills" of relational communication are missing in apologetics. We need a posture of both humility and confidence.

To get the Stump sessions started, we usually plant a question or two in the audience. This gets the ball rolling. Many students can't articulate their questions until they hear questions raised by others. Then their own questions start to crystallize, and they can speak up. It seems to me students are starving for a place to ask questions, though they may not realize this until they're in a setting where questions are being discussed.

Apologetics as a wrench

Think of evangelism as a toolbox that contains many tools, such as testimony, service, Scripture, asking brave questions, etc. Apologetics is one of the tools, like a wrench. So, whenever a nonChristian friend has a question, use the wrench. Answer the question as best you can, or tell the person you'll research the question and get back to them.

Apologetics is best weaved into conversation in a natural way. One of the skills of witness is to fluidly exchange tools in the toolbox at a moment's notice. So, I may be telling a story from the life of Jesus and my friend stops me to ask a question about the reliability of the

Bible. At that point, I switch over to the wrench for a while before returning to the story.

Do whatever works

Apologetics as a formal discipline is a complicated matter. One can talk about offering evidence for the faith, critiquing other worldviews, or defending the faith against attacks. There are also various schools of thought such as presuppositional apologetics, evidentialist approaches, and Reformed epistemology that may even assume God as a starting point.[18] Specialists should study all these models. But non-specialists should just do whatever works, whatever the occasion calls for. That's the beauty of thinking of apologetics as a tool of evangelism rather than a separate track that requires formal training and adherence to strict methodology. In other words, you don't have to be a professional plumber to use a wrench!

The best apologetic

One of my mentors in apologetics, the late James Sire (author of *The Universe Next Door* and many other books), always insisted that the very best apologetic for the Christian faith is Jesus. I mentioned this in Chapter 4 but it's worth repeating: *Every line of argumentation must eventually come to the identity of Jesus.* If Jesus is the unique revealed Son of God as described in the New Testament, everyone should bow down in worship. And if he's not, then all belief systems are up for grabs. So Jesus' question recorded in Mark 8:27 is perhaps the most important question of all time: "Who do people say I am?"

---

18   For an overview, see James Beilby, *Thinking About Christian Apologetics* (InterVarsity Press, 2011).

Three brief examples

Let's say that in the course of conversation over several months, a non-Christian friend asks the following three questions. My brief responses after each will at least suggest a direction for further discussion.

1. **If God is so good, why is there so much evil and suffering in the world?**[19]
   - **First, care:** As important as the philosophical questions are, we often just need to show care for the hurting.
   - **Broken world:** God gave us free will to love or reject him. Our rejection of God brought the whole world down, so that evil and suffering are commonplace in our experience.
   - **Positive Christian response:** We don't always know why bad things happen. What we know is that the people of God are called to work in the power of the Spirit toward healing and justice in this broken world (rather than wait for God to snap his fingers and make everything right).

2. **Why is there so much violence in the Bible?**
   - **Descriptive passages:** The Bible often describes violence (and violent characters) in a fallen world, but does not prescribe such violence.
   - **God's wrath:** A careful study of the Old Testament shows that God is extraordinarily patient with sinful, fallen people. It's only after persistent disobedience that God's wrath is expressed. [20]

3. **Why is the church against the LGBTQ community?**

---

19 For a helpful summary, see C. Stephen Evans and R. Zachary Manis, 2nd ed., *Philosophy of Religion* (InterVarsity Press, 2009), chapter 7.

20 See the Old Testament book of Jeremiah for many examples. For a broad, accessible treatment, see David T. Lamb, *God Behaving Badly* (InterVarsity Press, 2011).

- **Level playing field:** Anyone is welcome at church! The playing field is level: whether gay or straight, trans or cisgender, we're all sinners in need of God's grace.
- **Do you wish to be a disciple of Jesus?** (I find this question very helpful.)
  - If so, the Bible calls us to certain standards of sexuality.
  - If not, that is a different matter . . .

My further thoughts on apologetics are in an essay, here[21]

---

21   tinyurl.com/42hfra4f

GOSPEL OUTLINES AND CALLS TO FAITH

Motivation for calling others to faith

- We're called to be witnesses in the power of the Holy Spirit and to make disciples of all nations (Acts 1:8, Matthew 28:19).
- The harvest is ready! Workers are needed to share the message of Christ (Matthew 9:37-38).
- Jesus sends his disciples (that's us) out to "fish for people" (Mark 1:17).

Verbalizing the gospel

It isn't enough to witness with our actions, as important as that is. We must also verbalize the message. Paul seems to have this in mind when he writes, "How can they believe in the one of whom they have not heard? And how can they hear without someone preaching to them?" (Romans 10:14)

Remember that the reason we ourselves are people of faith is that someone verbalized the message to us. Now it's our turn to pass it on to others.

How to start explaining the gospel

There are multiple ways to begin. First, pray. Then, when the time seems right, simply ask if the person has heard a summary of the gospel message (or message of the Bible). If not, ask if you can share it with them. This process can be done with a stranger but more likely with someone with whom you've been in spiritual talks for a while.

Gospel outlines

It's helpful to have a summary or outline of the gospel message from which to work. Here are two:

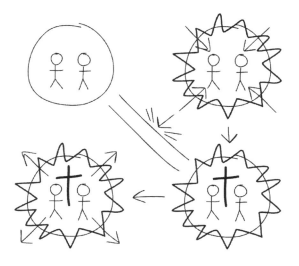

The Four Worlds[22]

The story can be told various ways. Here is one version: Top left circle: The world, our relationships, and each of us were designed for good. Top right circle: But all creation was damaged by evil because of our self-centeredness and inclination to seek our own good above that of others. Bottom right circle: But God loved the world too much to leave it that way, so he sent his Son, Jesus, into the world. Jesus took all evil with him to death on a cross, and through his resurrection, all of it was restored for the better. Bottom left circle: At the end of time, all will be fully restored, but until then, the followers of Jesus are sent out to heal people and the systems of the world.

---

22   Learn how to use the Four Worlds (Big Story) here: https://theministryplaybook.intervarsity.org/courses/sharing-the-gospel, or google "InterVarsity Ministry Playbook" and choose the free "Sharing the Gospel" course.

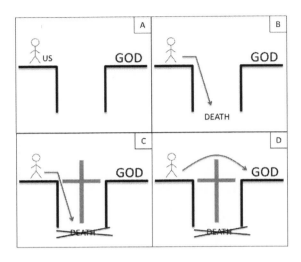

The Bridge[23]

Script: God created us to be in relationship with him as part of his family. But we rejected God and turned our back on him. The Bible calls this sin. Thus, we are separated from God, spiritually speaking. We try to get back to God through our own efforts but it is never enough. We cannot earn our own salvation. Because of his love for us, God sent his Son, Jesus Christ, to die on a cross to pay for our sins so that we can be reconciled to God. So the gap between us and God is bridged by the cross. The way to walk across the bridge is this: If we repent of our sins and place our faith in Jesus' teachings, death, and resurrection, we will be saved. Are you ready to cross the bridge and join the family of God?

---

23 For a better graphic see https://www.navigators.org/resource/
the-bridge-to-life/ or google "Navigators Bridge to Life."

Calls to Faith

- **Individual conversation:** At some point, we ask people if they're ready to cross the line of faith. A common way to put this is, "Is there anything preventing you from becoming a follower of Jesus"?

  Or, with a little more encouragement built in: "You sound like you're ready to become a follower of Jesus. Could I explain how to do that?" And then you share the Four Worlds or the Bridge, or simply explain the gospel message in your own words. A student at Texas A&M opened her Bible to John 3:16 and asked her inquisitive nonChristian friend, "What do you think this means?"

- **Small Group setting:** You can share a gospel outline with the group, or simply use a Scripture passage such as the "prodigal son" text in Luke 15 to call group members to faith. It's a good idea to tell the group ahead of time you're going to do this. After explaining the gospel, you can ask everyone to bow their heads, and simply ask if anyone is ready to become a follower of Jesus. If so, would they slip up their hand? Then pray for the new believers, and follow up immediately.

  There are many other ways to make a call to faith. Use your creativity! One idea is to incorporate the Five Thresholds and ask members where on the grid they find themselves and what their next steps might be.

- **Large Group setting:** Most speakers around InterVarsity these days make multiple calls to faith on a single occasion. The first call might be to Christians to reengage their faith and seek the Lord with all their hearts. The second call might be to those who've drifted away from the faith and need to recommit their lives to Jesus. Maybe they had a childhood faith that has been lost, and now they want to return as a believer. Or maybe they just need to make an adult decision about God in their life. The third call is to those making a first-time commitment. Be very clear about this. And on this third call, many speakers offer two opportunities. The first is a simple invitation. The second is prefaced with some Holy Spirit reassurance to those experiencing fear and doubt that may be holding them back from faith.

More suggestions for Large Group calls to faith

- **Soft approach:** Ask people making a commitment to slip up a hand while heads are bowed. Leaders must be watching from the front to see the response. I tend to use this approach in GFM.
- **Bolder approach:** Same as above, except ask people to stand when making any of the commitments. Then move them to the front for prayer. This has the advantage of immediate and public recognition of a faith commitment.
- **Commitment card:** This is a common and effective method for responders to specify their commitment, which may be to investigate Jesus further, join a small group, or make a first-time step of faith. A sample is below. Modify it for your context.

Responding to Jesus' Invitation

I'm exploring Christianity and:

____ I want to think more about who Jesus is, so I'd like to connect with others for more conversation.

_____ I want to use my words and commit to Jesus tonight, in response to his love and his deeds.

_____ I'm curious about what Christians do on campus. I'd love to connect with others this spring.

I'm a follower of Jesus and:

_____ I've been thinking a lot about Jesus and have significant questions. I'd like to talk more with someone.

_____ I want to grow in using my words to invite others to understand and experience Jesus' love.

_____ I want to grow in serving others on campus, personally, and/or with InterVarsity.

Large Group (cont.):

- **Warn of what's to come.** Notify the audience during the prior talk or music set, etc., that you'll be providing an opportunity in a few minutes to say yes to Jesus and join the family of God.
- **No coercion allowed.** I always tell students and faculty that this is an *invitation* to faith and that their response is voluntary. There is no pressure. If it's their time to start following Jesus, great! If not, that is okay. There will be more opportunities in the future.
- **Two key words:** Gentle. Clear. Especially in the grad world setting, we need to treat our audience with gentleness and respect and also be *crystal clear* about the gospel message.
- **What to say from the front** during the actual moment of commitment: This varies with different speakers. Some pray a prayer of accepting Christ, line by line, with new believers repeating each line to themselves. Others just pray a more

general prayer of affirming faith in the lives of those who are saying yes to following Jesus. I suggest: develop your own method and style. And remember to be both gentle and clear.

- **Followup!** Staff and/or a follow-up team must begin discipling new believers. An early step is to ask if they understand the commitment they've made, and walk them through the gospel message again.

FACULTY WITNESS

(an extended appendix)

Types

- Grad student sharing with faculty
- Campus ministry staff sharing with faculty
- Faculty sharing with faculty
  - · (note that "faculty" includes campus administrators as well)

Context

In general, nonChristian faculty tend to be skeptical about Christianity and the place of the church in society.

- **Modernist critiques** of the faith include scientific/empirical challenges to supernaturalism and thus the miracle claims of the Bible.
- **Postmodern critiques** focus more on the church's perceived role in issues of justice, oppression, colonialism, and politics.

Posture for grad students and campus ministry staff

Two words I keep hearing from practitioners of faculty witness are humility and curiosity. These qualities are indispensable, especially for grad students sharing with their Principal Investigators and other advisors. By contrast, preachiness and an attitude of superiority will be counterproductive.

- **Grad student sharing with faculty:** A PhD music student in Indiana entered into intentional conversation with her advisor, simply by asking questions. She began with professional questions about music and religion, then moved to deeper inquiries as the Lord opened the heart of the advisor to share about her personal beliefs and values. Discussions took place over a period of months.

  Despite the power dynamics in faculty-student relations, students sensitive to the Spirit can follow the Lord into spiritual conversation with professors.

- **Campus ministry staff sharing with faculty:** In Kansas, two staff called on a professor who met them in his office on a Friday afternoon, arms crossed. "What do you want?" he asked bluntly. "What are you selling? Show me your stuff."

  Through kindness, respect, humility, and curiosity, the staff gradually won the trust of the professor over a period of months. They asked about his calling into the field of sociology, and the conversation progressed from there. Note:

they were not maneuvering or manipulating the teacher into position for witness. They were *genuinely curious and kind.* The Lord opened a door. The professor eventually agreed to speak at a Pew-sponsored event on religious perspectives in his field. And his wife joined a campus ministry Bible study.

- **Faculty sharing with faculty:** Ariel, a professor of English at a large university in the West, recommends a posture of humility as well. She approaches colleagues with genuine questions about their professional lives, gradually shifting the subject matter to more personal items. This is the "onion-skin" method described in Appendix 3. Ariel told me that if fellow professors are willing to extend the conversation and disclose more of themselves, it's a sign that God is opening a door (Colossians 4:3). But if they aren't willing – well, *never force open a door.*

Of late, she has begun sharing with them what she's reading in the Bible.

Featuring faculty expertise

A common way of befriending and engaging faculty is to invite them to speak publicly in their field of expertise, or to use that expertise to comment on a related field. At a private school in Minnesota, an atheist philosophy professor did a wonderful job explaining and criticizing the boundaries between faith and science at a public event we held. As a bonus, I was able to meet with another atheist professor who was interested in the topic as well. We became friends and talked extensively about philosophical and spiritual matters. I asked him whether both progressive and conservative students have a voice on campus. He quickly asserted that in his classroom "all are welcome and encouraged" to speak up. I affirmed his openness as a professor, then asked about his own spiritual background, if any. He told me the story of his embrace of atheism in college, and I was able to share how I became a Christian – also in college. God was in that conversation.

Faculty Roundtables

One obvious opportunity for substantive dialogue with scholars on campus is the Faculty Roundtable discussions that began in 2002 and have been held at Harvard, Yale, MIT, Brown, Northwestern, Ohio State, and other schools. The stated goal of a Roundtable is to "foster cross-disciplinary community and dialogue among faculty that explores the intersection of current scholarship with various ethical, worldview, and religious or non-religious perspectives." Roundtable discussions often have a virtual option as well, making participation possible from remote locations.

The Critic

A campus staff in the Southeast told me a story of interacting with a strong critic of Christianity. It began at a public lecture when the speaker exclaimed, "White Christianity is the scourge of the earth!"
The staff continued his story as follows:

> Around the room, I witnessed discomfort and anger side-by-side with affirmation. I had never heard a public speaker make such a bald statement. While I was skeptical of the claim, I realized that I was also curious. I patiently waited for the crowd to disperse to greet the speaker, Drew, and thank him for his talk. "But there were some things you said that puzzled me," I added, "and I'm not sure I understood. Could we grab lunch sometime so I could hear more?"

Later, we enjoyed a delightful conversation as I explored his perspectives on European Christian history, missions, and the legacy of colonialism. I discovered, to my surprise, that we actually shared many concerns, and that Drew's critique sprang from a place of love – not only for the victims of historical injustices but for the "white Christianity" he called out so forcefully.

I also learned more about Drew – his background in the evangelical church and his journey away from faith in graduate school.

Several years have now passed. Drew's thinking continues to challenge my theological and spiritual life. I have cheered his awards, celebrated his achievements, lamented his disappointments. He has partnered in events and assisted me in ministry presentations. He invites me to sit in on classes. We continually discuss the gospel as I bring my questions and explore his critiques. My life and work are richer for knowing him, and I think I have brought an incarnational presence, enriching his life as well.

I love how the staff member's witness is integrated into the issues of life and not something artificially separate, as if "regular life" is over here and evangelism over there. Rather, evangelism is *embodied*. It's inside regular life.

Should we apologize for the church?

One veteran staff I interviewed thinks it's important to acknowledge and apologize for the church's sins of the past (and the present) when we talk with skeptical faculty. Such contrition helps break down barriers and builds trust. Again, posture and attitude are so important.

When we walk into the office of a faculty member we're saying, in essence, "I'm here in the name of Jesus to serve and care for you. Eventually, I hope to share God's message of salvation with you as well." This is the ancient *Shema* in action, of loving both God and neighbor (Mark 12:30-31). Included in that love is the longing for the person to become a follower of Jesus.

Does religion have a place in the university?

Are we legit? As Christians, do we belong on campus? A quick survey into the history of education in the global West shows Christians at the forefront of education in general, science and healthcare in particular, and even in advancing political-ethical values such as diversity and equality.[24]

I am concerned that Christians in academia fall into self-doubt and shame too easily. Fear of Christian triumphalism can set us back on our heels. At one school in the South, Muslim students are known to be kind and bold. I don't always see these qualities among Christians, who often project an image of self-reproach. There is a difference between humility (positive) and disgrace (negative). When I meet with a professor, I want to humbly acknowledge the flaws of the church (if necessary), but also proudly identify as a follower of Jesus. There is no shame in that (Romans 1:16).

Philosopher emeritus Nicholas Wolterstorff at Yale writes that God or religion is not an "add-on" to normal, secular life. Rather, we interpret all of life in a "certain way – *a theistic* way, if you will."[25] That is to say, we show up as Christian theists as our starting point.

---

24 Alvin Schmidt, *How Christianity Changed the World* (InterVarsity Press, 2004). See esp. chapters 4 (equality), 6 (health care), and 9 (science).

25 Nicholas Wolterstorff, *Religion in the University* (Yale University Press, 2019), 86.

We're under no obligation to first prove God and prove Christian legitimacy before proceeding to love and speak and contribute to the well-being and prosperity of the university (Jeremiah 29:7). Hence, we arrive on campus, implicitly or explicitly "in the name of Jesus," and our conversations with nonChristian faculty begin exactly at that point.

Kate Bowler witness

Many years ago, at Macalester College in Minnesota, I met a student named Kate. Within ten minutes of saying hello, we were talking Bible, theology, and church history – a conversation that lasted the next three years (and beyond). She was unusually sharp. She went on to earn graduate degrees at Yale and Duke and was hired onto the faculty at Duke Divinity School, where she serves as associate professor of the history of Christianity in North America.

At age 35 Kate was diagnosed with stage four cancer. Out of her arduous experiences of illness and navigating the health care system, she's written several best-selling books, and hosts the popular "Everything Happens" podcast. And she can be seen and heard on television and radio around the country.

I bring her name up because she's a remarkable evangelist. I doubt she would describe herself as such. She's never said that to me. The reason she's so effective at reaching a wide audience—both academic and popular—is that she's not trying to be an evangelist per se (that I know of). She's just being her very Christian self. Everything about her, whether it's suffering or scholarship, family or hobbies, is connected to God. Thus, she doesn't have to manufacture connections to the gospel for the purposes of "evangelistic" conversation. She embodies the gospel, often with humor. She writes of her Mennonite heritage as a "long line of overworkers, famous for pacifism, simplicity, and the foreboding sense that God is very disappointed by naps."[26] And of finding God: "If we are lucky, we see God in something really mysterious, like a miracle. But mostly we see God in regular surprises like love and forgiveness."[27]

I wish for such fully integrated spirituality for myself. And for you as well. It makes witness so much more natural. Kate seems to be saying to all of us, "Show up Christian. Own it. Acknowledge pain and doubt. Say something funny. Care. Serve. Share about yourself openly, in the name of Jesus. Amen."

26   Kate Bowler, *No Cure for Being Human* (Random House, 2021), 21.

27   Ibid., 132.

INTERNATIONAL STUDENT WITNESS

Goals of this appendix

- To highlight a few main principles of international student witness and ministry.[28]
- To point you toward more thorough resources.[29]

Note that about a third of all students in GFM are internationals.

---

28 Sources: a personal interview with Eva Glick (Nov. 28, 2022), InterVarsity Associate Director of Campus Integration (ISM); and the document, "Engaging Internationals – Discerning Your Approach." Google that title or link here: tinyurl.com/2bnef5kj.

29 For a wealth of information, simply google InterVarsity ISM, or the international student work of any campus ministry. A six-minute video that helpfully updates certain expectations of ISM is here: tiny.cc/is-gift.

International Student Ministry (ISM) basics of the past

- Hospitality: welcoming the foreigner into our midst with food, conversation, activities, transportation, shopping, move-in, etc.
- Friendship: showing the love of Christ.
- International students developed as future leaders back in their home countries.
- Bible study as a way to learn and practice English.

Emerging principles for ISM

- Reciprocal hospitality: dynamic giving and receiving of friendship, food, culture, and ideas between Americans and foreign students and faculty.
- Leveling of the playing field, less (if any) assumed deference paid to American culture.
- Social justice concerns: Activism among international students on the rise.
- Broad acknowledgment of past (and current) injustices worldwide, such as colonialism.
- Students emboldened in their home countries and in America to speak up.
- Increased commonality among students and faculty around the globe on issues of justice.

    "You can't just walk in and pretend that a lot of things didn't happen in the past." – Eva Glick.

- International students developed as disciples, not necessarily as future leaders (though some are).
- Varied backgrounds are more common these days, such as third-culture kids, immigrants, or students who come to the

U.S. for boarding school, then advance to undergrad and grad programs.

Example: Student A was born in the U.S. while a parent earned a PhD, then grew up in Nigeria, and is now back studying in the U.S.

Mistakes to avoid

- American paternalism: relating down to foreign students and faculty or treating them merely as "guests," thus diminishing or demeaning what they offer.
- Failure to understand nuances of cultural, ethnic, and geographic background of students and faculty. Need to learn individuals' unique stories.
- Confusing internationals with their ethnic American counterparts (ex: Korean vs. Korean American). Mistakenly assuming they have the same interests, culture, cuisine, language, etc.

  One Japanese American said to me, "People ask me where I'm from (Phoenix!). They tell me my English is good (It's my first language).
- Thinking that all universities have well-developed hospitality programs for students, including host families, plans for holidays, etc. That may not be true of your local campus.
- Using American cultural/geographic references in talks, ice-breakers, games, etc. A game played at one campus I visited required each person at Large Group to discover the name of an American figure (superhero, celebrity, cultural-political-historical icon) that was taped to the back of their shirt by asking questions of other participants. International students had little idea of these references and felt left out.

Suggestions for conversational friendship and witness

- Highly recommended: *Friendships with International Students Booklet.*[30]
- Slow down. Cross-cultural friendship and communication take more time.
- Be a learner. Take a humble posture.
- Use this question: Where did you grow up? Anyone can answer this.
- Not this question: Where are you from? This can be off-putting to American minority persons.
- Reciprocity: Give and receive! Cook for them. Then allow them to cook for you. Same with all cultural traditions. Mutuality is the key.
- Listen well. Learn the particularities of the other person. Don't assume they fit into cultural/geographical generalizations.
- Concerns for social justice may open doors for spiritual conversation or hinder it. Don't assume either way. Contextualize for each person. We're all on the journey together.
- Differentiate between Christianity and Western culture. Christianity is global, not American. "You have to help them see that Christianity is not a Western faith." – Eva Glick.
- Cultural curiosity doesn't always imply spiritual openness. A student or faculty may want to find out about American values and religion but may not be spiritually curious in their own life. Ask questions. Care. Use the onion skin approach of Appendix 3.

---

30 *Friendships with International Students Booklet* (tinyurl.com/5ahwxbfy)

- With Muslim students, a great tool to begin friendships is a Peace Feast, where a meal and spiritual conversation can be shared.[31]
- Expose them to testimonies from other internationals. This is helpful in showing that faith in Christ is a viable option for non-American students.
- Eventually, read Scripture together.[32] This is the most powerful tool of witness at our disposal. See Appendix 6.
- In some cases, it's best for students and faculty to read the Bible in their own language.[33] Many have never owned a Bible.
- Follow-up (re-entry) is vital but can be difficult. Connecting new believers to pastors, churches, and mentors back in their home countries must be done with care, and will likely take significant time. Too many international graduates drift from active faith when they return to the challenges presented by their home cultures and families. Starting social media (WhatsApp, Signal) groups of returnees is a great way to peer disciple.

Chapters and groups

- Different models of chapter configuration.[34]
  - ISM chapter: comprised mainly of international students.
  - Multinational chapter: comprised of an intentional mix of American and international students.

---

31 www.peacefeast.net

32 ism.intervarsity.org/resource/igig

33 tiny.cc/ibible

34 https://ism.intervarsity.org/engaging-internationals-discerning-your-approach (tinyurl.com/yhuvhzjk)

- Emerging multinational chapter: comprised of an unintentional mix of American and international students.

WITNESS TO BLACK SCHOLARS AND PROFESSIONALS (BSAP)

What is BSAP?[35]

BSAP IS A department of InterVarsity's Graduate Faculty Ministries.

The vision of BSAP is to see a generation of African Americans and people of African descent who are graduate students, faculty, and/or professionals being transformed by Christ, being renewed in their academic pursuits or professional lives, and becoming agents of transformation within the African American community, the church, and the world.

---

35   https://bcm.intervarsity.org/black-scholars-and-professionals-bsap (or google "BSAP InterVarsity").

Suggestions for white (and other non-black) campus ministry staff and student leaders[36]

- **Black diversity 1:** Know that black students on campus come from a variety of backgrounds, such as African Americans (Westerners, Southerners, Easterners, Midwesterners, etc.), African Caribbeans, African Canadians, African nationals, and Africans from other parts of the world. Some represent "majority" black populations, others minority (as in the U.S.). Students from different geographic backgrounds have differing interests, motivations, and racial experiences. Don't assume anything. Take time to know individuals for who they are.
- **Black diversity 2:** All black students are not the same. Some have grown up in white spaces and will navigate a predominantly white space comfortably. Others might appreciate help gathering other black students, perhaps to form a small group, but are less interested in participating in a predominantly white fellowship.
- **Go:** Find places on campus where black students hang out. Go there and make friends. Adopt the posture of a humble learner. Be intentional. Establishing cross-cultural relationships usually doesn't happen by accident. Prayer and persistence are required.
- **Mentors:** Look for black mentors, place yourself under black leadership, and be willing to take risks and make mistakes.

---

36   Sources: 1) A personal interview with BSAP Director Denise-Margaret Thompson. 2) Panelists Valerie Gladu, Don Paul Gross, Kevin Kummer, Howie Meloch, and Denise Margaret-Thompson in the webinar, "Being and Creating Welcoming Spaces for Black Students," https://youtu.be/8QGL9M9OOXE. 3) The Black Campus Ministries Resources page: https://bcm.intervarsity.org/resources (or google "InterVarsity BCM").

- **Black Cultural Center:** Find it on campus and meet the director. Attend their events and learn to care about the issues they care about.
- **Professors:** Network with black professors. They provide long-term continuity in the university and often know black students.
- **Trust:** Build trust gradually. Be patient. It takes time to overcome suspicions many black students have of (especially) white culture.
- **Take a personal interest:** The desire to incorporate black students into our groups or to support an autonomous black fellowship should not override personalized witness. Take a deep interest in students' backgrounds, families, churches (or lack thereof), education and career goals. Expect the onion skin approach to evangelism (Appendix 3) to take much longer in cross-cultural conversations.
- **Acknowledge the past:** In witness, be ready to verbalize the church's historic (and contemporary) complicity in slavery and racism. Acting like "that was then, this is now," as if nothing ever happened, will block relational trust and likely shut down the conversation altogether. A simple introduction to racism among the religious is Martin Luther King's "Letter from Birmingham Jail," which can be found all over the internet. One of King's criticisms is the lack of engagement and support from white pastors and churches on the racial issues of the day.

Chapter inclusion and development

- **Invite:** Reach out to black students twice as much. Practice the art of "loving persistence."

- **Welcome:** Make welcoming, incorporating, and developing black graduate students a non-negotiable priority. Invest yourself in personally following up new black students, making time to meet with them, inviting them to influence the group (in informal and formal leadership roles), and helping them navigate their experiences of racism.
- **Promote:** Invite black students to shape the character and culture of the group. As they are promoted to places of leadership and influence, they may become more comfortable, while white students (and others) become more *uncomfortable*. Be ready for these dynamics.
- **A tempering statistic:** Currently, more than half of GFM is comprised of students who are neither white Americans nor black. Thus, the dynamics of chapter diversity don't necessarily boil down to the white-black binary. Whatever the particular local ethnic mix is should shape chapter culture around food, music, worship styles, etc.
- Models of inclusion: Different methods of inclusion can be used in various contexts. Here are three approaches: a) Multiethnic chapter invites black students to integrate into its Large Group, small groups, and leadership team. b) Multiethnic chapter invites black students into designated BSAP small groups within the chapter. c) A separate fellowship outside the multiethnic chapter is created for black students, which would function as a more autonomous BSAP group.
- **BSAP at Stanford, as an illustration**
  - A few years ago, staff and student leaders prayer-walked the campus, asking God to empower black students and faculty in their departments. They also connected with the Black Community Services Center, the Office for Religious & Spiritual Life, and a local church.

- The fellowship grew when incoming students with a background in undergrad BCM helped launch an outreach to black graduate students.[37]
- 30 graduate students are currently on the mailing list, which meets Sunday afternoons on campus. Instead of running these meetings, staff help reserve rooms and provide food.
- Three principles from the Stanford model suggested by BSAP Director Denise-Margaret Thompson:
  - "Let the students do the work themselves." They are capable. Our job is to support, encourage, and train them.
  - Develop a feeder program between undergrad black students and BSAP. It takes a lot of administrative effort to track incoming black students to master's and PhD programs, some of whom may show up with excellent BCM training and experience from their undergrad days.
  - Use black alumni, volunteers, faculty, and clergy to build and support the group.

---

37   BCM is InterVarsity's Black Campus Ministry, which serves mainly undergrad students.

SUPERVISING EVANGELISM

Visioning, Lurking, Hiring

An interview with Susan Park, Associate Regional Director,
GFM Northeast

Visioning

When Susan served as Area Director for the Boston team, she began the evangelistic task with a sense of *holy discontent* with the Area's level of evangelism. Yes, some staff were working on evangelism, but the team's general focus had been on building up the chapters and providing pastoral care to students. Evangelism wasn't a high enough priority.

Adding to the mix was the all-too-common narrative around GFM in general that while undergrad evangelism is plausible and often successful, evangelism at the grad/faculty level is much more difficult.

Susan challenged the team. "If we don't put effort into evangelism, we'll never know if it can work. And given who we are as an organization, evangelism should be a primary calling for us."

To begin a new era of outreach, she asked every team member for something she describes as "very incremental and doable." All staff were to set aside ten minutes in each student appointment to talk about witness, including asking students to identify by name two nonChristian friends God might be giving them for the purpose of prayer and witness (what we call "2+" in InterVarsity), and placing them in one of the Five Thresholds.

This whole approach didn't require any new structure or additional meetings for staff, just a small but significant adjustment to what they were already doing. And Susan modeled it herself by taking a whole year in Area Team meetings to focus on intercessory prayer and evangelism coaching.

So, would the team buy into the new paradigm? Make a course correction?

Susan remembers, "Everything was on the line for me. I didn't know if I would have a job anymore. That's how much was at stake."

Fortunately, the team agreed to move forward in evangelism. And Susan still has a job!

Lurking

I'd never heard of the "ministry of lurking" until Susan dropped the phrase into our conversation. It resulted from the question, "Are you more likely to develop a comprehensive Area-wide strategy for witness, or work with staff who are already motivated for it and build out from there?" For the GFM setting, Susan believes in "change leadership" that works from the ground up. So even though she presented a vision to the whole team, she focused her energies at the start on staff who were "in motion" evangelistically. Their model and stories became a basis for spreading the excitement of witness to the whole team.

The ministry of lurking happened when she went to campus. She hung out at chapter meetings and social events, meeting students and looking for two kinds of people: nonChristians, and Christians interested in evangelism who could be encouraged and coached. She found both and entered into several relationships as either a witness or coach. "I wasn't there to take over chapters," she reports. "I was lurking around the edges in order to do the kinds of things I was asking my staff to do." This was possible, of course, because of the proximity of the Boston Area schools, whereas many ADs around the country don't have this advantage.

I also inquired whether staff were eventually expected to conform to one or two main evangelism strategies, such as GIGs or outreach meetings, or if variety was the rule. This got a mixed response. Susan is in favor of staff working within their strengths and interests, so they don't all have to do the same thing. A couple of staff have had success with Alpha, for example. That doesn't mean everyone has to do Alpha. Yet, Susan does want everyone to be regularly in the Scriptures with nonChristians – one way or another. That's non-negotiable.

These days the main unifying factor for the team around evangelism is the Area's Fall Retreat. Students and staff have developed the practice of inviting nonChristian friends and colleagues to the weekend, where three different calls to commitment are made: one to first-time faith, a second to further investigate Jesus, and a third call for Christians to witness to others. Of this last call, Susan speaks of the power of seeing over a hundred students on a single weekend stand and commit themselves to the ministry of evangelism back on campus.

Hiring

My final question was about growing the team. What is she looking for in new staff? Can they learn evangelism on the job if it's mostly missing from their track record? In a word, no. For Susan, deeds done in the past are the best indicator of future performance. So, she seeks to hire staff who have previously taken risks with nonChristian friends and practiced the ministry of evangelism. No "convincing" needed.

Conclusion

As we talked, Susan kept emphasizing "intentionality" and "telling stories of witness." As the old saying goes, *evangelism leaks*. It disappears if we don't work at it constantly. This, too, fits with our theology of witness of God going before us. God is constantly at work, inviting us to join him. Susan's goal is to be constantly and intentionally at work, responding to God with a hearty "yes" for herself and her team.

PS: Susan recommends the strategy used in the Midwest Region of GFM, called "3-2-1":

3: Every student and staff pray regularly for three friends and seek to witness to them. This is similar to the "2+" mentioned above.

2: Every chapter in the Region holds at least two outreach events per semester. These can be in the form of Large Groups, Fall Retreat, service projects, Veritas, Alpha, GIGs – whatever.

1: Every chapter issues at least one call to faith per semester. This is most likely done at Large Group, but of course, can take a variety of forms.

Faculty groups may wish to adjust these metrics to their context. The goal, in any case, is to be intentional each semester about outreach to colleagues.

Questions for supervisors

1. Assess the relative strength of your Area or Region in evangelism. What's going well? What could improve?
2. For improvement, what are your next two or three steps in leading your team toward increased engagement in witness (such as prayer, training, visioning, planning)?
3. Is there any way you get can involved on campus more directly, as Susan did?

MY EVANGELISM PROFILE

T HE PURPOSE OF MEP is to make evangelism easier and more natural for you by helping you identify your God-given design in witness. Focusing on your strengths will help you see more fruit in evangelism.

Instructions

Read through the 16 Roles below, and choose up to three that feel most natural to you. Record your responses in this handy Google form,[38] which will be automatically emailed to you.

(Check in with a trusted Christian friend to get their input into your Roles. Feel free to take the MEP as often as you wish.)

Optional: Schedule a 30-minute coaching call with Rick Mattson at rick.mattson@intervarsity.org

---

38   Handy Google form is here: tinyurl.com/2p9xkn7w

16 Roles in Evangelism

Choose up to three Roles that represent your God-given natural design in evangelism. Record your responses in this handy Google form, and you'll receive an automatic email of your responses. The Role (or combination of Roles) that you choose will represent your Evangelism Profile.

1. Apologist: Defending the faith

If you are a reader, critical thinker, and facts-based person, and if you enjoy teaching and the occasional friendly debate, you may be gifted as an Apologist. Apologists study and present well-reasoned arguments on many topics, such as the problem of suffering and evil, Christianity and other religions, sexual ethics, and evidence for the life and resurrection of Jesus.

Action Steps

- Read and study apologetics books and articles. Watch online speakers and debates, and listen to podcasts.
- Find nonChristian partners that will provide you with respectful dialogue on apologetic issues.
- Caution: You may be skilled at and enjoy case-making and argumentation. Be careful not to rely on argumentation for its own sake. Remember that God is the one who empowers witness and changes hearts.

2. Artist: Creatively sharing the message

Artists bring unique and creative ways of sharing the gospel. Many artists know that their God-given talents go beyond mere abilities, to being part of their very identity. If you have a passion for both art and evangelism, "Artist" may be one of your main roles.

Action Steps

- Study artists and their work in Scripture. God is the Master Artist, as seen in Genesis 1-2, Psalm 19, and other places. Examples of human artists include Bezalel and Oholiab in Exodus 31.
- Practice your craft! Become the best artist you can possibly be, to the glory of God.
- Gather with other Christian artists to produce content that will reach nonChristians. Art is often best practiced in community.
- Reach out to nonChristian artists. Talk with them about their art, and share yours with them.
- Caution: Continue to seek constructive feedback on your work and try not to take criticism personally.

3. Developer: Helping others grow into their full potential in Christ

Developers possess a *vision* for the success and flourishing of others. This could mean training Christian leaders and evangelists to become fruitful in witness, or helping nonChristians learn to live an abundant life in Jesus (John 10:10). As a Developer, you may also enjoy mentoring unbelievers through Bible study. Overall, you have a great vision for the salvation of others and their growth into their "best selves" as created by God.

Action Steps

- Seek mentoring relationships both ways: receive mentoring yourself from a mature Christian, and offer to mentor others in the faith.
- Read/study the Bible regularly with nonChristian friends.
- Caution: As tempting as it is to focus on developing Christians into their full potential as evangelists, don't "let yourself off the hook" by neglecting direct contact with nonChristians in your own life.

4. Evangelism Leader: Leading teams for witness

If you enjoy recruiting and leading gifted individuals toward team-based evangelism ministry, you are likely an Evangelism Leader. You tend to have a big vision for effective witness where each member of the team plays a unique role. You get excited about carefully planned outreach events, parties, or ongoing ministry to a neighborhood, demographic group, or college campus, all in a team format.

Action Steps

- Actively recruit gifted, talented people onto teams for effective outreach. Pick a target mission field, then cast vision to potential outstanding team members, and (as God leads) draw them into the project.

- Work to develop the talents and skills of each team member through coaching and outside training opportunities, enabling them to make their best contribution to your team.
- Caution: Don't forget to pay attention to personal witness with your own nonChristian friends.

5. Farmer/Sower: Scattering seed widely

If you love getting into multiple spiritual conversations over a period of days and weeks, you may be a Farmer/Sower. You don't just "go deep with a few," you extend yourself to everyone around you. If you meet someone on a bus or airplane, shopping mall or city park, they'll soon know you are a Christian. You may receive prompts from the Spirit to go and talk to certain people, ask them deep questions, or offer to pray for them.

Action Steps

- Create a lifestyle of meeting people, sharing the faith, and inviting others to take the next step. Cast the seed widely wherever you go.
- Become a great listener by listening "in stereo," that is, with one ear attuned to the person before you, and the other ear attuned to the Spirit. Continually ask God what he wants you to say and do in the present conversation.
- When God opens a door for deeper conversation, go for it! Go below the surface with anyone you can.
- Caution: Sometimes Farmer/Sowers can be overwhelmed by the number of conversations they have going on social medial or with friends and neighbors. Don't be afraid to set limits on the number of people you talk with.

6. Gatherer: Drawing a crowd

If you have a fun, outgoing personality and an abundance of friends and acquaintances, chances are you're a true Gatherer. For outreach events such as parties, Bible studies, speakers, concerts, service projects, movies—any event that depends on people showing up, you can serve as a catalyst. You love people, love to invite, love to connect, love to have fun. When you and the gang arrive, let the party begin!

Action Steps

- Meet people, invest in relationships and serve others so that you have a strong relational base when it's time to invite them to participate in events.
- Invest yourself strategically in events that will best serve your nonChristian friends. Not every opportunity is a call to action on your part.
- Caution: Don't forget to spend time with the Lord renewing yourself spiritually for the fun but sometimes hard work of being a catalyst and inviter.

7. Healer: Working toward physical and spiritual wellness

Healers believe God still performs miracles, whether instantaneous or over time. They love to see people brought to health and wholeness and are willing to enter the front-line trenches with hurting, sick people to see them healed. Healers often have strong faith and a firm commitment to intercessory prayer. They tend to work in teams and are marked by deep compassion for those who are suffering.

Action Steps

- Actively seek out the sick and broken. Pray for them continually. Healers often report that early in their ministry they don't see the hoped-for results. But persistence pays off as they gradually see God's power break through (You may wish to read the remarkable stories of Heidi Baker at Iris Global for inspiration).
- Pray in community. Find like-minded prayer warriors who believe in the ministry of healing. A context of faith and spiritual expectation across a whole community can be a powerful force for dedicated prayer.
- Caution: Don't forget to receive strength and renewal for yourself from the Lord, lest you get burned out in ministering to others.

8. Hospitality Evangelist: Hosting conversations

If you enjoy hosting people for parties, dinners, outings, or even for one-to-one conversation, you may be gifted for Hospitality Evangelism. You may be a natural at welcoming guests and drawing them into meaningful conversation. You love to invite people into a warm environment of food, decor, and background music; this is where you do your best work as an evangelist.

Action Steps

- Hone your skills of hospitality by practicing often. Create events. Create atmosphere. Create great food. Invite!

- Join together with others who enjoy hospitality. Share ideas, create group projects, and invite together around a common vision. Hospitality is a wonderful team sport.
- Caution: Sometimes the polite conversation of hospitality falls short of being evangelistic. With God's help and leading, be sure to move the conversation toward spiritual matters.

9. Prayer Warrior: Doing battle in the spiritual realm

Prayer warriors know the real battle is fought in the realm of "principalities and powers." They seek to break the chains of spiritual oppression that hold individuals and organizations in bondage. Prayer warriors go beyond devotional reflection in their prayer life to active intercession, spending much time standing against the powers of the enemy. Their weapons are love, truth, Scripture, and persistence in prayer. The setting could be behind-the-scenes intercession or battling it out in the trenches.

Action Steps

- Pray your way into spiritual warfare. Find strategic battlegrounds of resistance, oppression, and injustice. Pray missionally for the gospel to advance.
- Team up with front-line workers who are doing evangelism or other kingdom work. Support them in prayer. Your gifts plus their gifts can be a powerful influence for breaking strongholds and advancing ministry.
- Caution: Be careful of burnout. Intercession can be a demanding ministry emotionally and spiritually. Make sure you are "battle-ready" when you go to your prayer station.

10. Justice Advocate: Communicating Jesus through justice

If your heart burns for racial and economic justice, and you see Jesus as the hope of the world, this may be your calling. Justice Advocates go into the community and "call out" oppression and racism. They show tangible care for the poor, the sick, and the under-served. Justice Advocates believe and advocate for kingdom-of-God principles: the "first shall be last," the poor are blessed, wages should be fair, business and government leaders must be thoughtful and sensitive, and people will find salvation only through Jesus Christ.

Action Steps

- Enter the front-line trenches. Go where the action is. Roll up your sleeves. Meet people in person and advocate for their physical and spiritual well-being.
- Stay in community. Justice work is teamwork. It often involves coordinating a variety of resources, service agencies, and opportunities.
- Caution: Justice advocates usually have no problem thinking holistically about ministry. They know that God cares for the whole person. Be sure not to neglect communication of the basic gospel message, however, of creation, sin, and redemption through personal faith in Jesus.

11. Loyal Friend Evangelist: Reliable and always there

If you're the type of person who likes to invest yourself in a small circle of companions, you may be a Loyal Friend evangelist. Whereas

141

other Christians spread themselves widely among many acquaintances, you'd rather "do life with a few," using your gifts of faithfulness, reliability, and loyalty. You show up to every wedding, graduation, milestone, celebration, and birthday party of your life companions, and are committed to walking with them long-term as they gradually move closer to Jesus.

Action Steps

- Find a few close friends, some of whom are not Christians, to love deeply and faithfully for the long term.
- Pray for your friends and pray that God will open doors of opportunity to share the gospel message.
- Caution: Don't let your wonderful gift of loyalty prevent you from making new friends and even moving on from friendships that are not healthy or productive in God's sight.

12. Preacher Evangelist: Bringing the heat

If you love being in front of a crowd and preaching the gospel message in powerful, creative ways, God may be calling you to be a Preacher Evangelist. Most likely, words come easily to you, and you have a unique ability to hold people's attention while speaking. Perhaps you can feel the Holy Spirit surging through your voice when you're calling people to repentance and faith, and you long to see massive numbers of conversions to Christ.

Action Steps

- Seek out coaching and training to hone your speaking abilities. Ask for feedback. Watch yourself on video. Develop your craft.

- Find teammates. Find others who share your big vision for powerful, public events where you (and others) can share the gospel message and bear fruit for the kingdom.
- Caution: Being on stage in front of crowds comes with its own temptations of ego, performance, and power. Be sure to serve humbly before God and stay accountable with your ministry partners for proper attitude and posture while preaching (and after hours).

13. Servant Evangelist: Meeting needs behind the scenes

If you love serving the physical and spiritual needs of others, generally from behind the scenes, you may find this role a natural fit. Perhaps you enjoy helping others with their home projects, childcare, cooking, car repair, grocery shopping, homework, etc. You may be the "good neighbor" who sees what needs to be done across the fence or across the hallway, then goes ahead and provides. Such acts of service enable the Servant Evangelist to model the love of Christ and share the gospel.

Action Steps

- Observe carefully: who needs help? Know your skills and know where you can plug in to serve others.
- Do a great job. Be thorough, and reliable, and cover all the details. You want to build a reputation as a great go-to person when jobs need to get done and done well.
- Caution: Be sure to enter into spiritual conversation. It's tempting merely to "serve by example," but true evangelism goes beyond actions (as important as they are) to include words of eternal life.

14. Teacher Evangelist: Instructing others in the gospel

If you already think of yourself as a natural teacher, God may be calling you to a teaching role in evangelism. Many Teacher Evangelists thrive in public roles, delivering the message of the Bible to audiences in classrooms, podcasts, and seminars. Others prefer one-on-one or small group tutoring situations, which can be more personal and interactive. Either way, the Teacher Evangelist engages in research and preparation, then delivers quality content to the great benefit of hearers. Teachers are also known for their ability to do Bible study with nonChristian friends.

Action Steps

- Pursue training and coaching. Don't settle for being a mediocre teacher. Become great at the art of delivering Christian content to others. A teaching event well done will lead to more opportunities

- Explore opportunities for evangelistic teaching by creating content for social media, or signing up to teach an Alpha course, or simply doing Bible study with a nonChristian friend or neighbor.

- Caution: It's easy for Christian teachers to fall into the habit of working exclusively with Christian audiences. Find opportunities to teach nonChristians. This takes great intentionality and risk but is worth the effort.

15. Wise Counselor: Giving godly advice

If people regularly seek you out for friendship and advice, you may be gifted as a Wise Counselor. It may be that God has given you special insight into the lives of others, and a sense of timing about when to share your thoughts. You love to listen to the "whole lives" of non-Christian friends and acquaintances, and offer prayerful solutions or penetrating coaching questions. You tend to focus on the few rather than the many, since spiritual counseling can be very demanding emotionally and spiritually.

Action Steps

- Read, pray, study, prepare. When nonChristians seek you out, make sure you are equipped for the task. Learn to listen to the Spirit's voice as you're meeting with a nonChristian friend or client.
- Learn to integrate biblical wisdom into *all* areas of life. If a nonChrisitan friend comes to you with a money problem, connect your answer to Scripture. The same applies to issues that are relational, vocational, recreational, emotional — etc. No issue lies beyond the insights of God's word.
- Caution: In providing overall biblical wisdom for nonChristian friends, don't forget to share the gospel. Often, general wisdom can provide a bridge to the message of salvation.

16. Writer: Communicating the gospel through written word

Do you love to read and write? Are you fascinated with how language works? Rather than chat in person, would you rather write someone an email or letter? Christian writers create content for blogs, scripts, articles, and full-length books. Most write for Christian audiences, so there's a need for creative, well-researched pieces written for unbelievers. You can write stories, essays, arguments, blogs, scripts – whatever might serve as a credible means of sharing the Christian worldview.

Action Steps

- Start writing! Practice, practice, practice. Join a writer's club to develop your skills and make yourself accountable for deadlines and critique.
- Read great Christian content in your area(s) of interest, and emulate it. Start writing blogs, articles, books — whatever you wish — for nonChristian audiences. This can be a great ministry for a church or other Christian organization.
- Caution: As with other artists, it can be hard for writers to ask for and receive critique of their work. It's best to find trusted advisors who can provide helpful, honest, caring feedback on your work.

Recording your responses

Record your responses in this handy Google form, and you'll receive an automatic email of your responses (check your spam folder if the email doesn't appear).[39]

Follow-up

1. Share your Evangelism Profile with Christian friends who know you well. As you get their input, you may need to adjust your choice of Roles. Take the MEP as often as you wish in order to refine your Profile.
2. Read through each of your chosen Roles again, then begin carrying out the Action Steps listed under each Role.

---

39 Handy Google form is here: tinyurl.com/2p9xkn7w

3. Teamwork: Find someone with a different Evangelism Profile and begin praying and dreaming of what God wants you to do with your profiles working together.

Made in United States
Troutdale, OR
10/03/2023